T0374814

The Inbox

The Inbox
Understanding and Maximizing
Student-Instructor E-mail

Jennifer D. Ewald

SHEFFIELD UK   BRISTOL CT

Published by Equinox Publishing Ltd.

UK: Office 415, The Workstation, 15 Paternoster Row, Sheffield, South Yorkshire S1 2BX
USA: ISD, 70 Enterprise Drive, Bristol, CT 06010

www.equinoxpub.com

First published 2016

British Library Cataloguing-in-Publication Data

A catalogue record for this book is available from the British Library.

ISBN-13 978 1 78179 113 4 (hardback)
         978 1 78179 114 1 (paperback)

Library of Congress Cataloging-in-Publication Data
Ewald, Jennifer, 1970- author.
  The inbox: understanding and maximizing student-instructor email /
Jennifer D. Ewald.
    pages cm
  Includes bibliographical references and index.
  ISBN 978-1-78179-113-4 (hb) – ISBN 978-1-78179-114-1 (pb)
1. Written communication–Study and teaching (Higher)–Data processing. 2.
Electronic mail systems in education. 3. Academic writing–Study and
teaching–Data processing. 4. Communication in education–Data processing.
I. Title.
  P211.4.E93 2015
  378.1'7344692–dc23
                                        2015010612
Typeset by S.J.I. Services, New Delhi
Printed and bound by Lightning Source Inc. (La Vergne, TN), Lightning Source UK Ltd.
(Milton Keynes), Lightning Source AU Pty. (Scoresby, Victoria)

To my students whose e-mails always encourage me, challenge me, and keep me busy! I value and appreciate our electronic interaction. Keep filling my inbox.

Contents

CHAPTER ONE

Student-Teacher E-mail: An Introduction

E-mail in Academic Settings

The growing number of hybrid and online courses offered through distance education, the popularity of smartphones, and the universality of internet connectivity are just a few of the many factors that affect communication between university faculty and students in the twenty-first century. Though meeting during office hours, speaking in person after class, and talking by phone are still options, much communication between students and their professors occurs via e-mail. While it is true that many students now prefer texting and social networking sites for interacting with friends and family, e-mail continues to be a common form of communication in academic settings, particularly with instructors who may be understandingly hesitant or unwilling to provide students with their personal cell phone numbers or to 'friend' them on *Facebook*.

Interestingly, in 1993, during the early years of student-teacher e-mail, a university-level accounting instructor adopted what then was a relatively novel approach to communicate with students; he declared his course paperless and *required* students to communicate with him strictly through e-mail (Atamian & DeMoville, 1998). To ensure that students interacted with him electronically, the instructor forbade them to visit his office or contact him by phone. In the published study of this 'experiment', the student participants pointed to one limitation of the approach, a factor that would likely no longer be mentioned by the majority of North American college students: a lack of convenient access to computers off-campus.

Higher education in the twenty-first century is characterized by electronic communication in instructional contexts such as online courses and distance learning in which teachers and students may never actually meet in person; most, if not all, of their one-on-one communication takes place through e-mail, yet, very little is known about the nature of these usually private interactions.

Even in courses with traditional in-person meeting schedules, university faculty receive frequent e-mails from students for purposes that, a relatively short time ago, could be accomplished only during face-to-face oral interactions. On the one hand, it is true that students who feel intimidated in face-to-face conversations with a professor may find it less threatening to express themselves via e-mail (Bloch, 2002, Weiss & Hanson-Baldauf, 2008), but on the other, some students fire off poorly-written or ill-conceived messages, sometimes later regretting their inappropriate content or tone. The term 'flaming' has been coined to account for usually rash decisions to post or send nastily-written messages; that is, expressing 'a strongly held opinion without holding back any emotion' (Shea, 1994: 43). In educational contexts, students may compose such messages to protest a grade or to express personal opinions about a teacher or other school authority. Though faculty may have equally strong emotional reactions, they are always expected to reply to students' messages in a professionally appropriate manner but have little more than intuition and previous experiences to guide them.

E-mail and Faculty Issues

Though new faculty are extremely well-prepared in their fields and some receive pedagogical training specific to their respective disciplines, few receive detailed instruction about how to manage the variety of academic and interpersonal matters that surface in their inboxes. Nevertheless, to protect themselves professionally and to be effective in the classroom, faculty must develop a more thorough understanding of the complex issues involved in student-teacher communication. For example, among many other questions, how do students use e-mail to communicate with their instructors and what kinds of topics do they address? How do they make requests? Is there a pattern in students' absence excuses? What do they complain about? In the particular context of foreign language classes, in what language(s) do they choose to write their messages?

Some faculty bemoan the creative spelling and non-standard language used in e-mail while others report misunderstanding and even taking offense at the informalities that often characterize students' messages. The titles of a growing number of published articles reveal the sometimes problematic nature of students' e-mails or their approach to electronic communication in general. For example, consider the following: '"At Your Earliest Convenience": A Study of Written Student Requests to Faculty' (Hartford & Bardovi-Harlig, 1996); 'Cyberstress: Asynchronous Anxiety or Worried in Cyberspace – I Wonder if My Teacher Got My E-mail' (Crouch & Montecino, 1997); 'The Professional E-mail Assignment, or, Whatsyername@howyadoin.com' (Rife, 2007); 'R U Able to Meat Me: The Impact of Students' Overly Casual E-mail Messages to Instructors' (Stephens, Houser & Cowan, 2009); and '"Please Answer Me As Soon As Possible": Pragmatic Failure in Non-Native Speakers' E-mail Requests to Faculty' (Economidou-Kogetsidis, 2011).

These articles address many specific characteristics of student e-mail, all of which complicate the student-teacher relationship and potentially frustrate teachers. For instance, a professor's reaction to a student's e-mail request may be influenced by the student's degree of directness and acknowledgment, or lack thereof, of the imposition the request involves (Hartford & Bardovi-Harlig, 1996; Bloch, 2002; Economidou-Kogetsidis, 2011). Another potential source of frustration for faculty are students' explicit requests for a reply. Students' documented insecurities about the trustworthiness of technology to accomplish its task (Crouch & Montecino, 1997) have been significantly reduced over time; today, most e-mails reach their destinations and most attachments open easily, yet students continue to request that faculty respond to their messages (Economidou-Kogetsidis, 2011). These requests may simply reflect a need for confirmation or they may stem from previous experiences with teachers who did not reply. In addition, Stephens, Houser & Cowan (2009) found that faculty are also put off by e-mail 'violations' such as misspellings ('meat' for 'meet'), informalities (the use of 'R U' in place of 'are you'), and unsigned messages. Their study reported similar reactions from faculty of different generations. In fact, some professors are so concerned, or bothered, by what they perceive to be inappropriate messages that they purposely design assignments to communicate their e-mail expectations to students (Rife, 2007). Clearly, the discourse context of student-teacher e-mail is complex.

E-mail as a Hybrid Discourse Context

The informal and immediate nature of e-mail communication has given rise to unique discourse strategies implied by the article titles listed above. Though combining the norms of oral and written speech is often efficient, the resulting linguistic informalities can spark misunderstandings and interpersonal problems. Linguists have long categorized human communication as either spoken or written with specific interactions ranging from very formal and professional to abbreviations, acronyms and slang. However, it is commonly believed that e-mail discourse is not so easily classified as one or the other.

In 1998, Naomi Baron, a linguist interested in understanding language use in communication technologies, traced the evolution of human interaction over the last century, noting that people formerly had only two ways to communicate with each other: (1) face-to-face through immediate speech; or (2) across physical space and time via writing, that is, by letter or telegram, received and read by the recipient usually after the passing of time. She emphasized the absence of intermediate options, such as the 'new communicative modalities that blend the presuppositions of spoken and written discourse' (134). Now, with regular landline phones, technologically-advanced smartphones as well as computer-mediated video communication (e.g., *Skype*), people are able to communicate orally from a distance through immediate speech with or without seeing their interlocutors.

Technology also makes possible written communication in real-time through online chat rooms; in fact, one user's 'statement' can overlap the next resulting in complex turn-taking patterns among interlocutors who, in some cases, also have the option of seeing each other with the quick click of a button. The convenience and economic benefits of online chat appeal to many businesses, whose online customer relations departments offer clients a LiveChat option to manage any number of business-related transactions (e.g., purchasing a plane ticket, ordering a library book, hiring a plumber, changing from cable television to another service provider, etc.). Much is yet to be investigated in these real-time, or very near real-time, conversational contexts that, as 'LiveChat' implies, often sound spoken in register but are written in form.

Over the past decade, most researchers have come to the conclusion that e-mail is a kind of hybrid discourse context, characterized by both spoken and written communicative norms (e.g., Muniandy, 2002; Absalom & Marden, 2004; Chen, 2006; Crystal, 2006; Marques, 2008; Tannen, 2013). To illustrate, Muniandy (2002) defined e-discourse, including e-mail and Internet-relay chats, in hybrid terms, noting distinctive features such as the 'structural formatting of the message content, [certain] linguistic conventions ...[and] the use of short forms and symbols to convey meaning' (55). Looking more closely at actual e-discourse samples, one observes the parallels between e-mail and memos, particularly the structure of their fixed headers: the *To*, *From*, *Date* and *Subject* lines automatically supplied by e-mail systems (Crystal, 2006). Crystal highlighted several similarities between e-mail and other forms of communication. Comparing e-mails to informal letters, he emphasized senders' use of greetings and farewells, and in comparison with phone conversations, he noted the 'dialogue style' (Crystal, 2006: 130) that develops over the course of several exchanges. He also observed that stylistically e-mail can share the terseness of telegrams. Like others, he concluded that e-mail does not fall neatly into either the spoken or written categories and that it is a unique form of communication; depending on the context, e-mail can be both more or less efficient and more or less appropriate than phone calls and letters. More recently, Marques (2008) framed e-mail as a point on a continuum between spoken and written language, sharing characteristics with each while existing as a type of hybrid between the two. For example, among other characteristics, she claimed that e-mail fits somewhere between the turn-taking organization found in speech and the monologic organization of writing. In addition, she noted that though e-mail is often characterized by the lexical entries and non-standard grammatical features of spoken language, it can also include more prestigious vocabulary and the standard grammatical markers found in written language. Citing Crystal (2001), Marques (2008) stated, 'E-mail is an aspect of Computer-Mediated Communication [CMC] which has contributed to a new view of language and to the assumption of a new medium' (566). Finally, Tannen (2013) even drew specific comparison between pragmatic aspects of spoken discourse (e.g., expressions of enthusiasm, indirectness, pacing/pausing in turn-taking, etc.) and their technological counterparts (e.g., use of emoticons, repeated letters, electronic response times, etc.).

Research on Student-Teacher E-mail Interaction

Though there is a general consensus that e-mail shares features of both written and spoken discourse, this medium of communication continues to intrigue researchers from a number of academic disciplines. E-mail discourse is of great interest as well to educators who seek to understand several issues including why students choose to e-mail their teachers rather than avail themselves of other means of communication, how students and teachers view e-mail communication, what topics they address and functions they carry out via e-mail, and what linguistic features characterize their interaction. Given the frequency with which faculty and students communicate via e-mail, these issues are closely linked to developing effective student-teacher communication and, ultimately, to creating productive learning environments.

Research on student-teacher e-mail communication has identified a number of specific functions. Students have reported using e-mail for a variety of purposes (Waldeck, Kearney & Plax, 2001) such as clarifying assignments or course requirements, explaining absences, and requesting additional help or special accommodations. Other studies document teachers' use of e-mail with their students for the following reasons: to hold virtual office hours (Atamian & DeMoville, 1998; Biesenbach-Lucas & Weasenforth, 2002); to serve as a context for writing dialogue journals (Bretag, 2006); to serve as a medium through which students are required to submit completed assignments (Worrells, 2001); to carry out a service-related task (renting a car, making a hotel reservation, etc.) with students in a foreign language course (Garrido, 2000); to establish communication between foreign language students and native speakers of the target language outside of class (Pérez, 2000; O'Dowd, 2003; Itakura, 2004); to create a forum for tutoring in writing classes (Anderson, 2002); and to carry out small group peer review projects (Strenski, Feagin & Singer, 2005). To improve overall communication with an entire class, teachers were encouraged to set up list serves for their engineering courses (Hassini, 2006), a function that is now a feature of many online course management systems such as *Blackboard*, *Moodle*, *WebCT* and *Canvas*.

Researchers have analyzed students' e-mails using various categorization schemes that classify a message's content or purpose. For example, one study identified three categories: students e-mailed their teacher to clarify course material/procedures, as a means of efficient communication, and for personal/social reasons (Waldeck, Kearney & Plax, 2001). Another study used a four-category framework: student e-mails included content described as phatic communion, asking for help, making excuses, and making formal requests (Bloch, 2002). A third classification scheme identified students' e-mails as reflecting facilitative, substantive, and relational content (Biesenbach-Lucas, 2005). Samar, Navidinia & Mehrani (2010) suggested that students' e-mails were written for course related, personal/relational, and other purposes. Finally, many recent studies on e-mail communication refer to an earlier, extensive investigation, based on questionnaire data, in which students reported communicating with their instructors for 24 particular motives (Martin, Myers & Mottet, 1999). These investigators grouped students' responses into five main categories: relational, functional, excuse, participation, and sycophancy. That is, students claimed to communicate with their instructors to develop personal relationships with them (relational); they sought more information about the course material and assignments (functional); they offered excuses for late or missing work or challenged the teacher's grading practices (excuse); they demonstrated their interest in the course and their understanding of the material (participation); or they wanted the professor to view them favorably (sycophancy). Each of these frameworks offers researchers a particular perspective through which to investigate students' e-mails and the purposes for which they write them.

However, the communication analyzed within these frameworks has relational, professional and pedagogical consequences that are not as neatly compartmentalized. For instance, Sheer & Fung (2007) highlighted both the desirable and undesirable effects of e-mail interactions, noting their impact on students' evaluations of teachers and on student-teacher relationships. As mentioned previously, some teachers reported reacting negatively to those features of e-mail that characterize it as a hybrid form of communication. Stephens, Houser & Cowan (2009) found that teachers, more than students, reacted negatively to the absence of a sender's signature in the message closing or to language more often associated with texting. Glater (2006), writing for *The New York Times,* explained that teachers have reportedly been put off by students' messages that were 'too informal' or 'downright inappropriate'. He quoted one teacher who complained, 'The tone that they take in e-mail was pretty astounding. ... 'I need to know this and you need to tell me right now,' with a familiarity that can sometimes border on imperative.' (para. 5). He also cited teachers who claim to have felt imposed upon by students' e-mail requests to provide feedback on drafts of projects almost due. Other teachers have been annoyed by subject lines such as 'Respond Immediately' or by a message's ungrammatical content (Weinstock, 2004). Furthermore, pragmatic issues such as differing politeness norms have also negatively affected teacher recipients, though researchers attributed these differences to the native- or non-native status of the message senders (Hartford & Bardovi-Harlig, 1996; Biesenbach-Lucas & Weasenforth, 2002; Biesenbach-Lucas, 2005; Chen, 2006; Biesenbach-Lucas, 2007; Economidou-Kogetsidis, 2011).

E-mail Etiquette

As a result of their discontent and perhaps with a desire to provide students with valuable training, teachers in various disciplines have attempted to teach e-discourse etiquette or e-mail literacy. Based on their own e-mail experiences, some faculty are concerned that students may truly not know how to communicate appropriately in professional contexts; consequently, as educators, they accept teaching e-mail etiquette as part of their role. In the same *New York Times* article, Glater (2006) reported on a few professors who imposed e-mail rules and communicated those standards to their students. These stipulations included expectations for how quickly teachers would respond to students' messages, how the messages should be written in the first place, and which types of messages would receive a reply. Glater also cited a specific English professor who advised students to say thank you after receiving a professor's response. Ironically, this advice highlights the complexity of applying etiquette and politeness norms as some faculty may perceive such 'thank yous' as undesirable clutter in their already crowded inboxes.

Some teachers approach the matter of etiquette by conducting discourse analysis activities in class. Two English as a Second/Foreign Language (ESL/EFL) teachers asked their own students to create e-mail requests as samples (Mach & Ridder, 2003). The teachers then used those e-mails to illustrate the notion of pragmatic appropriateness as they together analyzed the messages' content; they gave students advice about writing e-mail requests, and asked students to work with partners to revise their own messages. These teachers focused specifically on students' overreliance on the word *please*, their lack of politeness strategies, and their positive use of if-clauses to acknowledge imposition on the part of the message sender. Though Mach & Ridder (2003) did not analyze empirical data, they claimed that this activity 'leads to some extremely helpful class discussions about cross-cultural differences (e.g., differences in the assumed obligations of teacher, differences in politeness strategies) that are the roots of students' pragmatic problems in English' (3).

Another teacher reported using a 'professional e-mail assignment' at the beginning of a first-year writing course (Rife, 2007). As part of this task, students read several texts ranging from online 'how-to' articles to more complex readings on multiliteracies and composition theory. They analyzed actual e-mails to identify their informal and formal characteristics and reflected on the implied relationship between the message senders and receivers as well as on the impressions particular e-mails might make on their recipients. Following the completion of this assignment, this professor reported two specific areas of improvement: she no longer received (1) e-mails lacking names or subject lines nor did she receive (2) e-mails whose entire message was conveyed in the subject line from these particular students.

Research on E-mail in Foreign/Second Language Contexts

In the specific context of foreign or second language teaching, the use of students' first (L1) or second (L2) language in e-mail communication with the professor reflects a controversial pedagogical issue. Methodological debates over the exclusive use of the target language in L2 pedagogy have prompted numerous studies of the role of the L1 and L2 in language classrooms (Turnbull, 2001; Storch & Wigglesworth, 2003; Macaro, 2005; Turnbull & Dailey-O'Cain, 2009). Though many teachers and researchers continue to emphasize pedagogical approaches that require maximum use of the target language in class, there is an increasing number of investigations that support the judicious use of learners' L1 (Antón & DiCamilla, 1998; Thoms, Liao & Szustak, 2005; Chau, 2007; Scott & De la Fuente, 2008). Nevertheless, excessive L1 use has been and continues to be consistently discouraged (Duff and Polio, 1990; Turnbull, 2001; Scott & De la Fuente, 2008), and though a growing number of researchers (Cook, 2005; 2012; Macaro, 2005; Edstrom, 2004; 2006; 2007; 2009; among many others) affirm the important role of the L1 in specific contexts, most current L2 teachers continue to value nearly exclusive target language interaction with learners.

The degree to which teachers expect learners to use the L2 beyond classroom walls, however, is unknown. Though some teachers prefer to interact predominantly in the L2 with students, even during office hours and on e-mail, others view out-of-class communication as an appropriate, and perhaps even necessary, site for L1 exchanges. Despite these differences of opinion, to date, few studies have systematically analyzed the language used in communication between second/foreign language learners and their professors outside the classroom.

Linguists are beginning to explore these and other e-mail related issues in both L1 and L2 contexts. Identifying rhetorical patterns, researchers have studied requests (Bloch, 2002; Biesenbach-Lucas, 2006) and excuses (Bloch, 2002), as well as analyzed the openings, closings and salutations of students' e-mails to their teachers (Sciubba, 2010; Economidou-Kogetsidis, 2011; Knupsky & Nagy-Bell, 2011). Others have investigated the link between particular linguistic features in e-mail and message content or native/non-native speaker status (Biesenbach-Lucas, 2005). Some investigations have compared the strategies used by native and non-native-speaking students for greetings and closings (Samar, Navidinia & Mehrani, 2010; Economidou-Kogetsidis, 2011) as well as their formulation of requests (Hartford & Bardovi-Harlig, 1996; Biesenbach-Lucas, 2007; Samar, Navidinia & Mehrani, 2010; Economidou-Kogetsidis, 2011). Most notable in all of these studies are the consequences, both demonstrated and potential, of students' e-mails on subsequent interactions and relationships with their teachers.

Absent from this growing body of research are large-scale, naturalistic, data-based studies that explore students' beliefs regarding e-mail communication, the written conventions evident in their e-mails, their use of the L1 and/or L2, and the rhetorical norms they employ for making requests, giving excuses, apologizing, complaining, and offering expressions of gratitude. All of these issues affect faculty reactions and responses, thereby affecting the student-teacher relationship and learning process. With a focus on moving toward a better understanding of students' e-mail beliefs and patterns, the following chapter outlines the research design of the present study and subsequent chapters explore in greater detail the topics listed above.

CHAPTER TWO

The Present Study: Research Design

Methodological Concerns in E-mail Research

Whether interactions are spoken, written or, as in the context of e-mail exchanges, 'hybrid' in nature, the challenges inherent in studying private communication are numerous. First and foremost are the complex and intertwined issues of participant privacy and data authenticity.

At first glance, it might seem that protecting participants' privacy necessarily involves sacrificing the quality of the data. For instance, one option would be to investigate e-mails composed by students who consent to take part in a research study. For data collection purposes, an investigator might give student participants the following prompts: 'Please write an e-mail to your professor to explain why you did not attend class and to request the homework assignment'; or, 'Please write an e-mail to your instructor to complain about the grade you received this semester.' But, the 'role-play' nature of this research task requires that students invent e-mails that they might on their own never choose to compose or address issues they voluntarily would not include in a real e-mail to their professor. This approach, though respectful of students' privacy, might result in misleading data.

Another approach would be to inform a particular group of students at the beginning of the semester that an investigation is underway and that any e-mail sent to their instructor over the course of the academic term could be included in that study; the researcher might even request the students' prior, informed consent to participate. Though the quality of these data would likely surpass that of the more 'role-play' e-mail data described above, this approach could still affect the naturalness and authenticity of the students' messages or, of more pedagogical significance, even restrain them from communicating by e-mail with their professor altogether.

These serious ethical and methodological challenges are inevitable in research on student-teacher e-mail interactions. Unfortunately, many published investigations do not specify how these issues were handled. Some research is based on natural data (i.e., real e-mails from real students) but no specific details are given about the research design and readers are left with questions about the ethical treatment of participants (e.g., was participant consent sought?; did students know their e-mails were being collected for research purposes?; how was privacy maintained?; etc.). Other investigations are based on elicited data (i.e., student e-mails written entirely for research purposes (like the aforementioned role-play situations) or composed by students who had been previously informed that e-mails would be collected for research purposes); in these contexts, researchers frequently provide a more detailed description of the data collection process and offer assurances that proper procedures were followed and that student participants gave informed consent. Any of these scenarios, though completely understandable from the perspective of research design, may compromise the quality of the data, call into question the integrity of the research, or both.

Data Collection in the Present Study

The present research was approved by its host university's Institutional Review Board for the Protection of Human Subjects in Research (IRB). This investigation analyzed 1,403 e-mails written by 338 students; these messages were sent to a university professor[1]/researcher over a period of 3¾ years during which time she taught 25 courses. The total enrollment in these 25 Spanish or linguistics courses was 421 students; some of these students took more than one Spanish course (e.g., Spanish I and Spanish II) or both a Spanish and a linguistics course over the 3¾-year period. Most, though not all, of the e-mails were written by students enrolled in the teacher's own courses; however, a small number of messages (fewer than 10%) came from the professor's official advisees or from students who sought information about study abroad, a particular course, or major/minor requirements. Students of Spanish (293) sent 1,193 messages; students of linguistics (39) sent 161 messages; and students enrolled in both Spanish and linguistics classes (6) sent 49 messages (information summarized in Table 2.1). The e-mails, in large part, were initiated by students though some were sent in response to messages they had received from the professor; e-mails in the latter category were included in the study only if the students used their messages to accomplish their own purpose(s) beyond that of merely responding to the professor's question. For example, in one

---

1   The terms 'teacher' and 'professor' are used interchangeably throughout this book and no distinction is intended by either term.

Table 2.1: Data Collection

Course	# of sections	# of students who sent e-mails	# of messages
Beginning Spanish	3	42 (12%)	1193 (85%)
Intermediate Spanish	6	90 (27%)	
Upper-level Spanish (conversation, composition, literature, culture or linguistics)	12	161 (48%)	
Introduction to Linguistics (taught in English)	4	39 (12%)	161 (12%)
Spanish and Linguistics courses	–	6 (2%)	49 (4%)
Totals	25	338*	1403*

(*percentages do not total 100% due to rounding)

case, the teacher e-mailed a student to request that he change his presentation date and the student replied answering only that question; his e-mail was excluded from the study. In total, from these 338 students and others, the teacher received over 150 e-mails that were excluded from this study.

The teacher's routine practice was to download and save all student messages in mail folders in *Eudora*, e-mail software stored on a personal computer. Thus, the e-mails constituted existing data; that is, the messages were not created or originally collected for research purposes, and, like other previously existing documents or records kept by teachers and school administrators, they were open to investigation provided that specific conditions were met to protect the identity of the students.

Though most service providers explicitly warn users not to expect privacy on e-mail, some students may still consider it to be a means for confidential communication. Therefore, one could claim that the present data collection method infringed on students' privacy because they sent these e-mails only to their instructor; moreover, the use of their messages for research purposes obligated students to be 'participants' in a study without their informed consent. However, the IRB that approved this project took several other factors into account. For example, first, the students' identities were already known to their teacher and, since their teacher was the researcher, their identities were never disclosed to a wider audience. In fact, as part of the analysis, each e-mail was assigned a number, and the students' actual identities became irrelevant. Second, appropriate changes were also made in the presentation of the data to alter any details that might make a particular student identifiable. Third, because students' written consent was not sought, there is no physical record (i.e., signed consent forms) that could be used to identify students. Fourth, the specific time period during which these e-mails were sent is not reported; additionally, not all e-mails received by the teacher during this time period were included in this study, further protecting students' identities. Fifth, students' e-mails were part of their academic record in the sense that they were saved for the purpose of establishing written documentation of the students' own excuses, requests, complaints, etc. in case the need arose to refer to their statements at a later date. And finally, following the analysis, the e-mails themselves were destroyed. In short, the case can be made that students' identities were not compromised by the study and that their unawareness of the research project strengthened the quality of the data.

This research design also offered the recognized advantages resulting from collecting natural, as opposed to elicited, data (Kasper & Dahl, 1991; Félix-Brasdefer, 2007; Ewald, 2012). In fact, many researchers (Hartford & Bardovi-Harlig, 1996; Biesenbach-Lucas, 2006; Demeter, 2007; Ewald, 2012; among others) who have conducted studies based on data gathered in both natural and elicited contexts claim that more investigations should be based on observational data. The debate between natural versus elicited data has existed since at least the early 1980s (Beebe & Cummings, 1996) and many researchers have acknowledged the advantages and disadvantages of both approaches to data collection (Rintell & Mitchell, 1989; Robinson, 1997Q1; Hartford & Bardovi-Harlig, 1996; Beebe & Cummings, 1996; Biesenbach-Lucas & Weasenforth, 2002; Félix-Brasdefer, 2003; 2007). On the one hand, elicited data techniques provide more opportunities to control social variables (Cohen, 1996; Beebe & Cummings, 1996; Demeter, 2007; Félix-Brasdefer, 2003; 2007). On the other, it has been found that these designed role-plays and discourse completion tasks (DCTs) foster unnatural behavior on the part of participants (Jung, 2004; Demeter, 2007; Ewald, 2012) which, in turn, can lead to invalid findings. In her study of e-mail requests, Biesenbach-Lucas (2006) pointed out that naturalistic data collection produces data that are not found through DCTs and, as a result, coding categories that were established to account for elicited data need to be revised. However, the analysis of natural data is often complicated by multiple social factors and a higher level of variation, but its great strength is in the authenticity of the human interactions observed. In one researcher's words, collecting natural data provides researchers a way to explore interaction in 'natural contexts where participants present their intentions with real-world consequences' (Félix-Brasdefer, 2007: 181).

These 'real-world consequences' are clearly relevant for students whose e-mails affect, both positively and negatively, the way their teachers evaluate both them and their academic performance. Given the hierarchical nature of the student-teacher relationship, any interaction is a potentially face-threatening endeavor (Hartford & Bardovi-Harlig, 1996; Biesenbach-Lucas 2007; Sciubba, 2010; Economidou-Kogetsidis, 2011). The e-mail context, inherently informal and often social in nature, further complicates what students may already perceive to be a highly unpredictable relationship. In short, role-play e-mails provide researchers with only artificial data, and even when elicited data are collected in contexts that are as natural as possible (e.g., from real students writing to real professors who know that their e-mails might be included in a research study), the results can be significantly different from those found in interactions with interlocutors who believe that their actions and words do carry real-world consequences (Ewald, 2012).

Participants and Context

The 293 Spanish, 39 linguistics, and six Spanish/linguistics students whose e-mails were included in this study represented various academic majors and minors. With only a few exceptions, they were native speakers of English who had lived all or most of their lives in the United States. As previously mentioned, their e-mails were written for authentic personal and academic reasons, they were saved by the instructor as part of routine practice, and no additional personal data was collected from the students or linked with their e-mails. Consequently, students' academic records, personal reasons for taking a particular course or section, future career goals, and other potentially useful information remain out of reach for this study.

Including the small percentage of students who were the professor's advisees, the students were ultimately enrolled in courses at the following levels: beginning Spanish (42 students – 12%), intermediate Spanish (90 students – 27%), upper-level Spanish conversation, composition, literature, culture and Spanish linguistics (161 students – 48%), as well as an introductory linguistics course (39 students – 12%) taught in English and six additional students (2%) who were enrolled in both Spanish and linguistics courses (see Table 2.1). Though most of the e-mails were sent while students were enrolled in their respective courses, some students sent e-mails during the summer or over the December break. These students all attended the same private university whose undergraduate enrollment was around 4,000. This institution offered both undergraduate and masters' degree programs in the humanities, natural and social sciences, and business. It attracted primarily middle- to upper-class, white students whose high school academic records and standardized test scores are average or above. Though some students in this study were Spanish majors or minors, many others were enrolled in Spanish courses only to satisfy the university language requirement. Most of the students who took the introductory linguistics course did so to satisfy a university course distribution requirement, a state requirement for English teacher certification, or an elective.

Data Analysis

As in investigations by Hartford & Bardovi-Harlig (1996), Atamian & DeMoville (1998), Bloch (2002), Poling (1994), Biesenbach-Lucas (2005), Bretag (2006), and Hassini (2006), among others, the present researcher was the teacher to whom these students sent their e-mails. The e-mails constitute 'data from authentic inter-actions... available for analysis without the presence of the researcher [or students' knowledge of a research study being underway] biasing the data collection process' (Herring, 2002: 145). Though for other methodological reasons some may criti-cize a study in which the teacher and researcher are one in the same, this common research design provided an additional safeguard for protecting the confidentiality of the students' identities as well as serving as the basis on which other related information would be accessible (i.e., classifying an e-mail as written by a Spanish or linguistics student; identifying a message sender as a 'Spanish 101' student or a Spanish major or minor; etc.). In sum, the benefits gained from basing this research on real students' e-mails, composed voluntarily for authentic purposes, far outweighed any potential disadvantages or limitations.[2]

The data analysis involved several steps. First, each of the messages was num-bered. A multiple-stage coding framework was devised that included the following e-mail content/function categories: attendance-related issues, dropbox, request, excuse, apology, complaint and thank you. An additional category was also added to analyze students' e-mail expectations. Because students frequently sought to accomplish multiple goals in the same message, there are many instances in which more than one of the coding categories applied. For example, a student's message sent to apologize for missing a class was often coded as 'attendance-related' and 'apology'. If a message contained a reason for an absence and a question about a missed homework assignment the e-mail was coded as 'excuse' and 'request'. Finally, if that same message included a statement such as 'Please respond as soon

2 It should also be noted that the analysis benefitted from the outsider observations of an IRB-approved researcher from a different university who did not know the students involved; she contributed greatly to five conference presentations of preliminary anal-yses of these data (Edstrom & Ewald, 2006a, 2006b; Ewald & Edstrom 2006; 2008; Ewald, 2013). Students' confidentiality was protected throughout this collaboration.

as possible' or 'I know that you probably won't see this e-mail until tomorrow', the message was also counted in the category of 'student e-mail expectations'.

Within some of the content/function categories, other relevant information was also noted. For example, within attendance-related e-mails, other features were recorded such as the presence of apologies, excuses and offers of amends as well as the timing of the e-mail (sent before or after the actual absence) and any student acknowledgment that a message had been sent on short notice or as a reminder of a previous interaction. Offers of amends sometimes called for the teacher to respond (e.g., 'would you please let me know if I should hand anything in?'); others did not (e.g., 'I will make up the work I missed and I got the assignment from my friend.'). In addition, many attendance-related messages reflected concern about protecting the student's relationship with the professor evidenced by closing statements meant to mitigate or soften the situation: 'Hope you understand' or 'Hope that's okay'. Finally, requests were classified as either directed toward specific information (e.g., 'what page was the homework?') or aimed at something else (e.g., 'please send me the document'; or, 'would you write me a letter of recommendation?'). Some of these requests included an expression of thanks as part of the message. All of these e-mail characteristics were tracked in the analysis.

Three other features were coded and analyzed. First, students' self-identification, or lack thereof, was tracked in the analysis. For instance, some students explicitly identified themselves in their e-mails with statements like 'This is Mary from your Spanish II class on M/W/F at 1:00'; other students left it to their teacher to identify who they were by name alone.

Second, stylistic features such as non-standard spelling and vocabulary were also noted in the coding scheme. These included abbreviations (e.g., 'u', 'w/', 'btw' and 'I need a sharp kick in the #!?'), capitalization (e.g., 'i' instead of 'I' or 'MANY problems') and other written forms of intonation (e.g., 'sigh', 'Yay!', and 'sooo much') as well as emoticons (e.g., '=)' or ':o)') and informal language (e.g., 'poppop' or 'the printer spazzed on me').

Finally, the students' choice of language(s) was also noted. The teacher did not require students to use a particular language on e-mail and, as a result, some wrote messages entirely in English, others entirely in Spanish and some in a mixture of both. (While some of the 39 linguistics students did know some Spanish, most did not; thus, writing e-mails in Spanish would not have been an option for them, and their messages are excluded from that part of the analysis.) Like the messages written in English, the small percentage of messages written only in Spanish underwent a detailed analysis including the identification of the message function(s) (e.g., request, excuse, expression of gratitude, apology, complaint) as well as the students' incorporation of other elements (e.g., well-wishes, confirmation).

In addition to expanding the existing literature on the functions and features of student-teacher e-mail communication, this study also furthers the boundaries of linguistic research on pragmatic functions by documenting authentic communicative exchanges between interlocutors via e-mail, a context that has received relatively limited research attention. The analysis of these e-mails focuses on the following topics, each of which is addressed in a separate chapter (chapter # listed in parentheses): student beliefs regarding e-mail communication norms and written conventions in student e-mail (3); students' use of the dropbox (4); requests (5); apologies (6); excuses (7); expressions of gratitude (8); complaints (9); and student use of the L1/L2 (10). Finally, the results of this study highlight the multidimensional role of students' e-mails and point to several implications for pedagogy in both L1 and L2 contexts. These findings contribute to educators' and linguists' understandings of the discourse strategies associated with e-mail and have implications both for electronic communication and for student-teacher communication in general.

CHAPTER THREE

E-mail Communication: Student Beliefs and Conventions

Hi Ms. [Teacher Name],

Sorry to bother you but I was just wondering if you could please give me the next assignment that we have to do for Monday. It would help me out so much because I have a very busy weekend. If you could please get back to me, I would appreciate it. Thank you so much for your time and have a great day! Sincerely, [Student Name][1]

The Importance of Understanding the Student Perspective

There are a variety of adjectives that could be used to describe student e-mails: engaging, sincere, informal, pushy, and offensive may provide a fairly representative sample. When it comes to discussing student e-mail, many faculty focus on emotional reactions rather than on actual data that indicate how students view electronic discourse. Often, faculty members exchange stories about unusual or even insulting messages they have received from students who, whether deliberately or inadvertently, made requests too directly or presumptively, used harsh or needless words to complain, and even apologized in ways that came across to their professors as shallow or insincere. Faculty members also complain about the non-standard features abounding in many students' e-mails, either worrying that students 'don't know better' or bemoaning what they perceive to be an overall lack of respect communicated through misspellings, ungrammatical syntax or overly

---

1   Throughout this book, e-mail examples are presented as they were originally written with only minor revisions, most aimed at protecting students' identities. Capitalization, punctuation and spelling are usually left intact regardless of their accuracy.

informal language. Published reports of such faculty complaints are plentiful (Hartford & Bardovi-Harlig, 1996; Weinstock, 2004; Glater, 2006; Biesenbach-Lucas, 2007; Stephens, Houser & Cowan, 2009; Economidou-Kogetsidis, 2011; among others).

Interestingly, Tannen (2013) specifically addressed the negative feelings some of the older generation has toward young people's use of online communication in general. She referred to it as a 'widespread the-sky-is-falling alarm' (100) and noted that the accompanying panic and scorn are illogical given that young people use electronic language in much the same way that spoken and written language have always been used. She illustrated her view with several interesting examples. However, many teachers, perhaps especially those who are less comfortable with current technologies, might disagree.

In contrast with some faculty members, traditionally-aged university students are particularly comfortable with technology and are highly accustomed to interacting with friends and family using instant messaging, texting, and, at times, e-mail. In fact, one often hears university students report that they rarely make phone calls to anyone but prefer to use their cell phones primarily for texting and web-based communication on *Facebook, Instagram* and other social networking sites. According to an article by Matt Richtel (2010) in *The New York Times*, young people say that the problem with e-mail is 'that it involves a boringly long process of signing into an account, typing out a subject line and then sending a message that might not be received or answered for hours. And sign-offs like "sincerely" – seriously?' (para. 5). Moreover, most social networking sites have revised their message services to make them seem more like texting to their users. Richtel (2010) reported that *Facebook* eliminated subject lines because their own in-house research found that they usually were either left blank or contained unhelpful entries such as 'hi' or 'yo'. According to *Inside Higher Ed* reporter Steve Kolowich (2011), Mark Zuckerberg, *Facebook's* founder, predicted 'We don't think a modern messaging system is going to be e-mail.' Nevertheless, Kolowich also reported that executives at *Google* and *Microsoft*, popular student e-mail providers, have not found significant dips in student e-mail use in higher education contexts; they expect the use of e-mail to continue in university settings, at least for a while.

One guiding assumption of this book is that an understanding of how university students view and use e-mail with professors might help faculty members accept, or at least better manage, e-mail interactions with their students. As reported, college- and almost college-aged students view e-mail as slow, boring and formal; in contrast, some teachers on the receiving end of their messages are bothered by e-mail's informality and abbreviated spellings (Richtel, 2010). This situation illustrates many of the difficulties both faculty and students encounter when communicating with each other in cyberspace. Given their respective – and different – starting points, it is predictable that some students will hurry through messages decorated with creative spellings and abbreviations, ask professors to respond quickly, and down play their language to avoid the formality that they dislike; and, unsurprisingly, some faculty members will negatively react to what they perceive to be students' impetuous tones, careless writing styles and overall lack of respect in the messages they receive.

Though students are using e-mail less frequently with friends and family members, it continues to be a common medium of university communication. As a result, some professors go to great lengths to make their e-mail expectations clear to their students; for example, they design extensive assignments to teach students what they consider appropriate e-mail etiquette and include detailed information on course syllabi to explain their e-mail 'rules'. But, as students write their professors to clarify assignments, explain absences, request additional help, and submit documents electronically, they continue to annoy, and even offend, some teachers. For as long as e-mail remains a popular medium of communication, faculty members will do well to adapt to changing styles if for no other reason than to be able to challenge the students' perspectives and behaviors they dislike.

Recent research has supported the incorporation of more 'pedagogical interventions' (75) focused on teaching appropriate student-professor e-mail interaction, especially when it comes to language learners' e-mail speech act production (Biesenbach-Lucas, 2007). Li (2000) and Bloch (2002) also advocate classroom activities or assignments focused on the development of student e-mail practices. Biesenbach-Lucas (2006; 2007) further encourages researchers to investigate a broad array of instructional types to determine their effectiveness in helping students compose appropriate messages to their teachers. As a result of improving pedagogical practices and solidifying institutional standards, she states, 'professors may eventually no longer write email etiquette rules into their syllabi' (76). She also emphasized that e-mail pragmatic expectations may pose problems even for native English speakers due to the hierarchy involved in the student-teacher relationship. She explains, 'while native speakers have the linguistic flexibility to manipulate language in the written medium to mitigate requests, they do not always do so, and run the risk of, unintentionally, conveying status incongruence' (2006: 101).

It is probable that the medium for university-level electronic communication will eventually change (Kolowich, 2011); therefore, a more thorough understanding of the current gap between student-teacher perspectives will put faculty members in a better position to respond to e-mail now as well as to react to future changes and even be active players in whatever new technologies arise to replace current systems. Stephens, Houser & Cowan (2009) note that 'as instructors are added to students' *Facebook* pages, for example, and engage in more social networking with students outside the classroom, it will be important to test the effects of these new instructional media relationships. If we are to teach students how best to use email, it appears that we must consider how their generation views technology and adapt our teaching methods to reach this population' (321–22).

Before adapting our particular methods, we must develop an acceptance of, or at least tolerance for, common student e-mail behaviors.

The present investigation revealed several expectations students hold for electronic communication. It might come as a surprise to note that students do indeed possess a general sense of e-mail rules (though they may disagree with their teachers on particular details); moreover, students also seem to recognize certain norms related specifically to student-teacher e-mail interactions. However, this analysis of their messages also revealed the e-mail behaviors that continue to frustrate teachers. For example, as will be seen in the subsequent sections, students' high degree of directness or their failure to acknowledge explicitly that a request entails at least some level of imposition (Hartford & Bardovi-Harlig, 1996; Economidou-Kogetsidis, 2011), their use of informal language, including abbreviations and emoticons, (Stephens, Houser & Cowan, 2009), their directives, both explicit or implied, to their teacher to reply to their e-mail (Hartford & Bardovi-Harlig, 1996; Economidou-Kogetsidis, 2011), or the imperative tone with which they sometimes communicate last-minute requests (Glater, 2006) could prompt teachers to react negatively. By examining samples of student messages, this chapter explores shared areas of understanding among students' and teachers' perspectives on e-mail as well as highlights possible points of divergence. In addition, this chapter emphasizes the need for teachers to approach e-mail with a measure of understanding of students' situations and e-mail style.

Students' Recognition of General E-mail Etiquette

This section of data analysis is qualitative. Thus, there are no calculations of frequencies with which students wrote particular comments or used particular words nor claims of statistical significance. In fact, in exploring students' beliefs, the goal of this chapter is not to make any specific assertions about the present data. Rather, repeated comments in these students' messages provide a window into their perspectives on the general use of e-mail, and the aim is to point out common trends and raise issues related to e-mail norms and to student-teacher communication in general. The issues highlighted here offer educators questions on which to reflect personally, and serve as suggestions to investigators of particular areas for future empirical study. Teachers are invited to consider student e-mails they themselves have received and to determine for themselves the relevancy and importance of these issues in their communication and relationships with students.

It is likely that not all students share the views highlighted in this section; indeed, not all of the students in this study made these or similar statements. In fact, since in previous studies students themselves reported that part of their communication with their professors is motivated by a desire to demonstrate interest in the course material, develop a relationship with teachers and, in more colloquial terms, earn 'brownie points' (Martin, Myers & Mottet, 1999), no matter their frequency, e-mail statements alone should never be used to ascertain what students believe about any issue. Their opinions and motives are complex and intertwined.

That said, there was evidence in some students' comments that they recognized the existence of what some have termed 'e-mail etiquette' (Pirie, 2000; Hassini, 2006; Weiss & Hanson-Baldauf, 2008; Economidou-Kogetsidis, 2011). Though their actual practices could aggravate some teachers, many of these students' messages pointed to their awareness of certain 'e-mail rules'[2] even as they simultaneously violated them. In many of these examples it is interesting to note the presence of the word 'but'; when used by students whose e-mail comments point to their awareness of an e-mail etiquette norm, 'but' seems to be the preferred transition for explaining why they are breaking the rule or expressing the purpose(s) of their message. The following sections are organized around some of these rules.

Rule #1: Don't Send Too Many E-mails or Long, Rambling Messages

Some students seemed to believe that one should not e-mail a recipient too frequently or that messages should not be too long and wordy. Their comments included the following: 'I'm sorry I constantly email you but...'; '...I know this is a long email, but...' and 'Sorry about the rambling'. Their acknowledgment of this norm should be of some encouragement to faculty members who tire of receiving messages containing seemingly convoluted questions or endless requests. As they subsequently did in these particular cases, students themselves often explain in these same e-mails that these messages spring from their own heightened levels

---

2   In this analysis, 'rule' and 'norm' are used interchangeably and are defined together as those generally unstated yet user-shared principles by which e-mail behaviors are governed.

of anxiety over difficult situations they are experiencing, worry regarding class schedules, or stress associated with completing degree requirements. Though in many cases their actual e-mails were, as they themselves claimed, frequent, long, and rambling, they sent them anyway, often with a 'but', breaking norms of e-mail etiquette that their own words acknowledged.

Rule #2: Don't Send a Recipient the Same Message Multiple Times

Apparently concerned about the possibility of breaking a different rule, other students explained why they sent the same message multiple times, an action they realized could be annoying to the recipient. This student explained it well: 'I have tried emailing you but my email has been down. None of the emails I send are actually going out I don't think.' Afraid that the teacher might be put off if indeed she had received the previously-sent messages, this student added, 'I could be completely wrong though'; she then continued with the reason for her e-mail. Violating the shared expectation that one should wait for a recipient and not push for a response, this student was careful to explain her action and attempted to justify having sent the e-mail in case her teacher had taken offense.

Rule #3: Don't Send Unreasonable Requests Last-Minute By E-mail

As reported by Glater (2006), many faculty members understandably object to receiving last-minute requests for assistance by e-mail, especially those that entail significant effort on the part of the teacher. Students' seemingly oblivious disregard for their instructor's time or their unreasonable expectation that an e-mail will be seen and its request addressed in short time or at odd hours often surprises faculty members. However, not all students share or communicate this expectation. Many of these students expressed awareness that it was unlikely or even impossible for the professor to respond to their last-minute messages or to those sent in the middle of the night, especially when class was to take place the very next morning. Moreover, others expressed recognition that there are questions that, for various reasons, should not be asked. For instance, these students sent the following e-mails at unusual times:

> Sent on Sunday at 10:45 pm: 'I **just** have a quick question about the exam. I may be crazy (or thinking of another class) but did you say we could use a

dictionary for the exam? I can't remember if it was for this class or not. If you don't get back in time, that's fine, I was **just** curious. Gracias, hasta mañana. [Thank you, see you tomorrow.]'

Sent at 2:12 am on the exam day: 'I know this is kind of late for an e-mail, but I studied for the test for a good amount of time today and then again tonight at the library. ...[she relates a story about a roommate's parent who had just died]... If it is at all possible that I could [take] the test at a later time I would greatly appreciate it. If not, no big deal, but I **just** don't want this test to greatly influence my final grade if I do poorly. If you get back to me before class tomorrow that would be great, if you don't get this until later I'll **just** tell you I guess when I get there. Thank you so much for understanding.'

Sent at 10:15 am on the class day: 'I was **just** trying to do the last part of the homework where we have to use websites to answer the questions, and I am having trouble getting on a few of them. I was **just** wondering if the addresses are wrong, or maybe some of the pages have moved? If you get this before class **just** let me know. Thanks and I will see you soon!'

Sent at 9:05 am prior to class at 10:00 am: 'Señora- It's about 9:05 right now- I'm not sure if you'll check this before class. But just in case, I wanted to let you know that my class registration for [the school to which I am transferring] is at 10 am eastern time, and that I'm going to be a bit late for class. If the quiz is at the end like usual, I most likely won't miss it. See you later.'

These students' 'if' statements (e.g., *if you don't get back in time; if not, no big deal; if you don't get this until later; if you get this before class;* and, *if you'll check this before class*), along with the *'But just in case,'* clearly communicated their awareness that their teacher was not always available on e-mail and their understanding that their requests might not have been manageable. In contrast to students who seem to lack respect for their teacher's time and make unreasonable requests last minute, these students made it explicitly clear that they recognized limits regarding what the teacher was able to do for them. Moreover, students' use of 'just' seemed to be aimed at softening requests and appearing reasonable if the instructor did not, or was not able to, respond. In addition, it seems as though these students recognized a certain risk in e-mailing their teacher at odd times but something else compelled them to go through with it: perhaps a desire to have gone on record for trying to notify her in advance or a belief that their below-par performance will outweigh the possible risk.

The e-mail norms mentioned above (frequency in number, length, content, patience in response time and reasonableness in request) are relevant to most e-mail communication, not only to student-teacher interactions. The next section focuses on particular issues related specifically to e-mails sent by students to teachers.

E-mail Rules Related Specifically to Student-Teacher Interaction

Some of these students also made comments revealing norms related specifically to e-mail interaction with teachers. Though faculty often express concern that some students do not recognize that e-mailing a teacher is not the same as e-mailing a friend (Biesenbach-Lucas, 2006; Chen, 2006; Rife, 2007; Stephens, Houser & Cowan, 2009; Sciubba, 2010; Economidou-Kogetsidis, 2011), several students' comments reflect their, perhaps surprisingly, nuanced understanding of the student-teacher e-mail context. The following sections are organized around some of these student-teacher e-mail rules.

Student-Teacher E-mail Rule #1: Don't Bother Teachers With Requests

Unless an e-mail contains a request for a relatively substantial favor, it would probably be somewhat unusual for a college student to e-mail (or text) a peer, starting off the message with 'I am sorry to bother you but...'. Nevertheless, many students used this phrase to begin e-mails to their teacher. Some of these messages did contain relatively significant requests to reschedule an exam or to write a recommendation letter, requests that entail considerable inconvenience, time or energy on the part of the professor; but, other e-mails included this phrase even when a message's purpose was simply to submit an assignment electronically or to ask a question about a homework assignment. Similarly, another phrase commonly used to preface a request was 'if you're not too busy'. Even in non-request e-mails and request e-mails involving minimal imposition on the teacher (i.e., the request falls clearly within areas of teacher responsibility and requires very little time to address), most of these students were careful to demonstrate respect for the teacher's position and time. In addition, common closing phrases included polite sign-offs such as 'Thank you for your time' and 'Thank you for your time and consideration'.

Since students in this educational context, and presumably many others, are encouraged to communicate with their instructors through e-mail, it is of some concern that many seemed to feel the need to start a message with such deference that they, in effect, apologized for 'bothering' the teacher as a part of making minor requests and asking questions. Most of their requests were, in actuality, very appropriate and fell within the boundaries of their teacher's responsibilities. It is very possible that literal interpretations of their opening phrases and what could be exaggerated understandings of their significance are unwarranted; students' use of these phrases could merely be evidence of their awareness of the hierarchy that exists in the student-teacher relationship, the norms of e-mail etiquette, and specific pragmatic routines associated with making requests. But, it is also possible that students' use of these phrases resulted from previous experiences with teachers who were inexcusably 'bothered' by student requests and questions or, unfortunately, who behaved as if they indeed were 'too busy' for their students. Their teachers' business may even extend beyond e-mail norms to include behaviors that communicate that the teachers are too busy for office hours, too busy for talking before or after class, and so on. If this seems an overstated interpretation of these students' comments, consider the hesitancy evident in the following student's e-mail as he indirectly made a request, explained why he was asking, specified that there was 'no rush' and that it was acceptable if the teacher didn't want to comply, and finally expressed appreciation if she could indeed grant the request: 'I was wondering if you could e-mail me what I got on the Spanish test because I just want to assess where I am at in your course. There is no rush so even if you don't want to do it, it is fine, but if you could I would really appreciate it.' Though students' linguistic expressions of respect for their teacher may be admirable and appreciated, faculty should always remain sensitive to the hierarchical disadvantage students face when interacting with professors and do their best to meet students' needs without capitalizing on this lack of professional equality, acutely perceived by at least some students.

Student-Teacher E-mail Rule #2: Don't Send Teachers E-mails When They Are 'Off-Duty'

On a very practical level, some students expressed awareness that teachers receive numerous e-mails and one even thanked his teacher for reading his messages: 'I'm sure you get many emails like mine at this time of year, and I appreciate you taking the time to read mine.' Others were careful to acknowledge in their messages that they were sending an e-mail at a time that their teacher might consider herself to be off-limits to students (e.g., summer, spring break, right after an exam, while attending a conference, late at night, etc.); many included apologies as part of their requests. For instance, 'I'm sorry to bother you in the middle of your summer but ...'; 'I'm sorry to bother you over break but ...'; 'I know we just took the exam, but I am concerned about my performance – especially if I am hoping to bring up my grade. I was just wondering what you think on this? Sorry to bother you so early after the exam.'; 'I know you are on your [conference] trip, but just in case you check your email at all, I have a question about the final project.' In all of these examples, again note the students' use of the word 'but' to transition from acknowledging what they perceived an e-mail etiquette norm to explaining why they were violating it.

This perceived rule 'violation' could have less to do with students' sending the actual e-mails and more to do with their understanding regarding when, in general, it is appropriate for students to make requests. It could be that e-mail was merely the chosen medium of communication in these particular instances and that the violation they perceived was most closely related to the timing of the requests themselves. Certainly it is a teacher's prerogative to establish and even announce times when they are 'off duty' and will not reply to messages. That does not mean, however, that it is inappropriate for students to send e-mails during those windows. Indeed, one of the benefits of this technology is the ability to communicate whenever it is convenient without waiting, for instance, for the daytime hours during which phone calls are considered appropriate. Sending a message while a particular issue is on one's mind merely puts the ball in the recipient's court. However, the same rights belong to all users and recipients can choose when it is convenient for them to reply. Students should know and experience, or be taught explicitly or through exposure, that teachers reply to e-mail during appropriate windows and within reasonable lengths of time but students should not be made to feel like it is inappropriate to send e-mails when they believe their teacher might be on vacation, at a conference, or otherwise occupied.

Student-Teacher E-mail Rule #3: Don't Resend Messages To Teachers Known To Respond Promptly

Some students' comments revealed that they had established certain expectations for e-mailing this particular teacher. For example, one offered an explanation for resending a message, basing his action on his familiarity with this teacher's e-mail habits. In the absence of a return message from his teacher, who had established the expectation of a relatively quick response time, this student was worried that some kind of technological error had taken place and resent his message around 11pm. Along with his attached composition assignment, he explained: 'I'm resending this because I thought I'd get a response from you but I never got one.' In contrast to the criticism potentially implied by his statement (specifically, 'you did not respond to my first e-mail'), his remark attempted to justify his violation of this e-mail rule. E-mail records show that the teacher replied to his second message at 8:30am the next morning, telling him that she was glad he resent it because she had never received his initial e-mail. Apparently, the student's concern that some kind of error had taken place was well-founded. Thus, rather than reacting negatively to this type of remark about not having received a response to an initial message, a teacher might interpret it as a compliment from a student who actually is expressing trust and security in a teacher's normal pattern of e-mail behavior.

Student-Teacher E-mail Rule #4: Don't Tell Teachers To Reply To Your Message

Most of these students' e-mails did not include explicit statements asking or directing the teacher to reply. Thus, in general, these students did not seem to believe that it was necessary or appropriate to tell their teacher to respond to their messages. But, these data did seem to indicate that some students had likely experienced negative e-mail patterns with teachers. Seemingly aware that some teachers simply do not answer e-mail or that significant time may pass before they receive a response, some of these students included explicit requests for the teacher to reply even after a couple of months of becoming familiar with this particular teacher's normal pattern of e-mail behavior. Some of these requests were very direct while others were phrased more indirectly; also, many students included politeness markers such as the words 'please' and 'thanks', verb modals like 'would', and time-sensitive phrases such as 'at your earliest convenience', 'as soon as you can' and 'asap' to soften their requests (however, Economidou-Kogetsidis (2011) pointed out that time expressions like 'asap' can be considered abrupt by those who do not view the expression as a softener). Consider the following statements, generally ranging from the direct to the more indirect:

'Please get back to me.'

'Please return this email to me at your earliest convenience.'

'Please e-mail me back at your earliest convenience.'

Please write me back and let me know! Thanks for getting back to me!'

Please let me know as soon as you get the chance!'

'I would really like to meet with you and discuss my pursuit of a minor...

'I would greatly appreciate a response as soon as you can.'

'If you could get back to me asap I would appreciate it very much.'

'If you could please get back to me I would appreciate it.'

'If you could possibly get back to me, I would really appreciate that.'

Finally, one student simply ended her message with this abrupt closing: 'Please reply, [Student Name]'.

Hartford & Bardovi-Harlig (1996) and, more recently, Economidou-Kogetsidis (2011) investigated e-mail requests, emphasizing the particular challenges faced by non-native speakers of English whose linguistic ability and politeness norms differ from those of their native English-speaking counterparts. Native speakers of English typically use more politeness markers while non-native speakers are more likely to include fewer indirect moves along with more linguistic markers that aggravate their requests (e.g., imperatives, an emphasis on the urgency of the request, and complaints or criticisms). Their research highlighted teachers' negative, or potentially negative, reactions to these types of pragmatic failures.

In the present study, many of the students whose 'please respond' requests were expressed more emphatically or directly and, thus, according to previous research, were more likely to receive negative faculty reactions, might have understood that they were breaking an e-mail etiquette norm. Evidence for this is found in their surrounding comments. Many of their e-mails explained the motives behind their direct requests for the teacher to reply as soon as possible; without such justification, these statements might otherwise be interpreted as impolite or aggressive.

For example, facing the possibility of not graduating on time, one student explained, '... all of a sudden, I feel like I may run out of elective space and time.

What do you suggest?? Please get back to me as soon as you can.' Her urgent tone was repeated in a message from a student who was 'desperately trying to find a Spanish class that fits [his] schedule'. He explained that the registration system had prevented him from enrolling in the appropriate course the year before and, having just found out that he was registered for the wrong level, he wrote, 'Presuming that I had my schedule intact, I went out and got a much needed part-time job over the break. Now, your class is the only time-slot ... which will allow me to fulfill my Spanish minor requirement and keep my job. Could you please e-mail me back as soon as you can this weekend? Thank you so much.' A third and final example comes from a student who did not attempt to hide her desperation at all. Her message began with 'I have a huge problem!!' Following these repeated exclamation points, she explained that her academic advisor had suggested that she seek a promise from the teacher, her current instructor, to sign her into a class that would likely fill before her turn came to register. She emphasized her desire to be a Spanish minor, her preference to continue studying with the same instructor, and the complications involved in completing the minor if she was ultimately unable to register for the next course. She wrote, 'My advisor told me that my only hope would be to see if you would sign me into the class if it is full which it most definitely will be by the 19th. I'm not sure what the rules are or what you want/can do, but he told me to beg you because it is my only hope. Please email me back at your earliest convenience. Can you help me, senora??????? Desperately, [Student Name]'.

These three students' explicit requests for fast e-mail replies, one during a weekend, could be perceived as pushy and, as described by a teacher in Glater (2006), 'with a familiarity that can sometimes border on imperative' (para. 5). Indeed, current research consistently reports faculty members' understandably negative reactions toward some student e-mail and often focuses on how best to teach students, both native and non-native English speakers, to communicate more effectively by sensitizing them to professional and academic expectations of e-mail politeness. But, it is worth remembering that students, like faculty members and everyone else, at times face issues that threaten their sense of security and well-being. Faculty members should remain aware of and sensitive to the reality that students' needs are sometimes, unavoidably, time-sensitive and that this situation often prompts them to compose less-than-polite e-mails, written in haste at stressful moments. Though not all poorly-conceived messages are born in such crises (for indeed, the poor quality of some messages is due to the students' ignorance of general politeness norms), some students send e-mails without having paid sufficient attention to issues of tone because of their heightened emotional reactions to their current situations.

In short, there are certainly cases in which faculty's negative reactions are justifiable and students may need more training in e-mail etiquette to be applied even in stressful situations; however, this analysis showed that many of these messages did reveal students' recognition of the importance of certain e-mail norms. The detailed explanations that accompanied students' urgent requests for their teacher's response, perhaps constituted attempts to justify indirectly their norm violation. Teachers should also entertain the possibility that a student's 'please reply' comment might be due to previous negative e-mail experiences. Thus, though inappropriate, the comment is not necessarily directed at the current teacher and, therefore, should not be taken personally. Finally, teachers should develop additional strategies for sensitizing students to the potentially negative effects of including such direct requests to reply.

Breaking E-mail Norms Without Explicit Explanation

In contrast, the messages of other students broke various norms of e-mail etiquette without any explicit justification or explanation. For example, the following message was written on a Friday by a student who already planned to visit the professor face-to-face during her office hours on Monday morning. He wrote, 'My name is [...]. I am interested in minoring in spanish. ... [He asked multiple questions regarding program requirements]. I register for classes on Monday at 4:30 pm. I stopped by your office today and saw your office hours [on Monday morning] so I will be in to meet with you then. But if you could please answer some of my questions ahead of time, it would ease my weekend a bit! Thanks again, see you Monday!'

Despite this student's probable anxiety over his registration appointment, his final phrase 'it would ease my weekend a bit!' seems to communicate a selfish lack of respect for the teacher's time. As reported in Glater (2006), faculty might be tempted to ignore such a message or to respond with annoyance. But, doing so would cause the student to miss out on an e-mail learning opportunity. In this particular exchange, e-mail records show that the teacher responded in about an hour to the student's message, briefly addressing some of his questions and reminding him that they would talk in person on Monday prior to his registration time, a context more appropriate for discussing such in-depth issues. The tone of this student's final reply was enthusiastic and his expression of gratitude specifically addressed the speed of the teacher's response: '... Thank you very much for your quick response. See you soon.' Trying to make this kind of situation a teachable moment is probably the best a teacher can do. It is unknown if this student learned anything about e-mail or not from their exchange. Indeed, e-mail etiquette is acquired over time and with experience. And, unfortunately for the student-teacher relationship, a large part of students' e-mail etiquette development actually takes place on e-mail and not through assignments or in response to syllabi statements and teacher lectures regarding appropriate e-mail conduct. But, as tempting as it may be at times, responding in annoyance, or not at all, to a student's unjustified violation of an e-mail rule does not positively contribute to the student's understanding of appropriate e-mail norms, nor does it maintain the professional integrity of the teacher. Moreover, some students have had the unfortunate experience of trying to visit a professor during office hours only to find the teacher absent or unavailable. Given this particular student's upcoming registration appointment, even this brief interaction with the teacher and the assurance of a Monday office hour meeting seemed to successfully alleviate his anxiety, and 'ease his weekend a bit'!

Another student sent a message that perhaps should have been canceled. Prior to handing in the final draft of an assignment, she wrote, 'Dear Dr. [Teacher Name], A little question. I want to know if you would prefer a folder instead of the green portfolio that I handed in to you the first time. I have both, so tell me which is more convenient for you.' Appearing to ask a superficial and perhaps ridiculous question, this message might annoy faculty members who tire of responding to student e-mail and replying to seemingly trivial questions. Once again, it is worth noting that students bring their past experiences to their internet interactions. It is possible that this student had previously studied with a teacher who was particularly selective about the format of a written assignment. If the student, or someone she knew, had lost points or suffered a loss of face over having submitted a paper in an undesirable format, for her, this question was anything but ridiculous or trivial and her e-mail request deserved a polite and helpful response. In fact, in her message the student herself acknowledged that she was asking 'a little question', perhaps a recognition that her question might not be terribly important in the grander scheme; nevertheless, it would seem unreasonable or even unfair to evaluate negatively her desire to conform to the teacher's expectations and to criticize her for asking the question, even if these types of questions take time on e-mail. A heightened sense of professional status might prompt teachers to think that they are above these kinds of questions and, thus, are entitled to ignore or respond negatively to messages such as the one described here. But, a sense of professional integrity should also encourage them to examine issues from the student perspective and, if they are so motivated, to use these moments to help students gain to a better understanding of e-mail etiquette.

Though most of these students' e-mails communicated respect for their teacher's time and other responsibilities, the following message contains problematic language that might reflect unreasonable expectations. The e-mail was sent on a Thursday, February 23, by an undergraduate student who was working on a research project for a senior thesis: 'Here is the [document] we have made up for the [committee]. If you could take a look at it whenever you get a chance that would be great. please take your time, we are not in a rush. if we could get your comments back by saturday or sunday that will give us enough time to make necessary adjustments before submitting on March 1. thank you so much for your help.' Though the student offers the teacher the opportunity to take her time and claims not to be in a rush, note that the teacher had only a weekend to provide comments on the research project. Also, the student reserved the greater portion of the remaining time for herself to revise the document and submit it to her committee by the March 1 deadline, approximately a week later. For faculty members who are annoyed by written capitalization violations, this e-mail contains additional sources of concern or aggravation. But, it should be noted that the teacher had previously committed to collaborating with this student and was expecting to review her draft; the student composed this e-mail with that understanding in mind. Thus, before reacting to a student's e-mail tone, it is important for faculty members to take into account that students send messages based on their understanding of previous interactions they have had with their teachers but do not always fully articulate their recollections. Indeed, they expect their teachers to remember what they told them previously, an assumption that is actually quite reasonable.

Some teachers are more willing to respond to a student in need especially if they know the student personally in some capacity. But, faculty advisors, program directors, and department chairs frequently receive e-mails from students who are unfamiliar to them. The following message was sent at 5:40 pm from a previously unknown student who asked multiple registration questions and requested that the teacher respond. After listing his questions, he wrote, '... I am registering tomorrow at 8 am so please respond when you receive this e-mail.' Understandably, faculty reactions to this kind of message will likely be less than favorable.

Somewhat in contrast is the following e-mail from a known student who had a scheduling problem regarding an exam taking place the next day at 10:00 am. Her message was sent at 9:13 pm. She also asked her teacher to respond, but in a different manner: '[She explained the scheduling conflict]... So, I just wanted to see if it was alright if I came a bit late tomorrow. ... If it's a big problem, just let me know by tomorrow morning-I'll check my email when I get up. See you tomorrow, [Student Name]'. Her request for a quick reply comes across somewhat differently since she provided softeners such as 'I just wanted' and 'a bit late'; her tone was more neutral though the time between the message and her deadline was actually shorter than that of the student with registration questions. Moreover, the level of imposition involved for her teacher to respond to her request was quite different from that of the previous situation. Responding in writing to a long list of student registration questions requires considerably more time than giving permission to a student to arrive late to class. Nevertheless, perhaps the most problematic issue is found in this student's final statement: 'I'll check my email when I get up'. This declaration seems to attempt to obligate the teacher to respond by e-mail since the student's phrasing implies that a lack of response by the next morning might be, in essence, understood as the teacher's permission that she arrive late.

As difficult as it sometimes is, teachers obviously can and should take time to step back and emotionally disconnect from student e-mails that, at least on first read, seem disrespectful, aggressive or even offensive. Slower reactions can lead to an improved ability to sympathize with and even understand a student's perspective and situation. Though some student e-mails are indeed inappropriate, rather than overreacting to a student's carelessly-chosen word or poorly-timed phrase, generously considering the context in which it was written can help faculty members understand and reply in appropriate and helpful manners. In addition, faculty members who do not distance their students because of their distaste for students' e-mail behaviors are in the fortunate pedagogical and social position of being able to expose students to more effective ways of communicating their needs and desires and encourage them to revise their e-mail habits.

Student Conventions in E-mail Communication

Previous research has already thoroughly documented several conventions evidenced in student e-mail. For example, investigations have measured the relative frequencies of particular forms of address (Economidou-Kogetsidis, 2011), greetings and closings (Gains, 1999; Rod & Eslami-Rasekh, 2005; Marques, 2008; Samar, Navidinia & Mehrani, 2010; Sciubba, 2010), and written irregularities including typos, non-standard vocabulary, grammatical inaccuracies, punctuation that communicates expressivity, and informal language (Baron, 1998; Absalom & Marden, 2004; Weinstock, 2004; Chen, 2006; Stephens, Houser & Cowan, 2009).

The present data do not represent exceptions to these findings. These students' e-mails contained greetings that ranged from 'Hey' to the considerably more formal 'Dear Dr. [Teacher Name]'. In between were 'Hi', 'Hey, Dr. [Teacher Name]', 'Professor' and 'Dr. [Teacher Name]'. In their e-mails, all kinds of written irregularities were evident such as 'Phew!!', 'Yay!', 'Haha' and 'MANY problems'. More comical were requests such as 'I just typed my comp in [the Spanish word processor] but its not showing any kind of corrections. I think I did something wrong.

What do you think?'; statements like '...I will be writing my professor [to complain] after my grades have [been] put through the resistors office'; and absence excuses such as '...I dont feel any better yet. I will give you a note from the nurse about my abstinence if I dont make it [to class]'! As are popular in other e-mail and texting contexts, students included many emoticons to express certain emotional reactions such as fear, unhappiness and contentment including:o, = (, and :-).

Many of their messages were decorated with highly informal and even ungrammatical language, representing both the e-mail communication context as well as generational styles. For instance, to express their actions, emotions and problems, students used phrases such as 'I googled and Ebsco-hosted', 'I was freaking out just now searching for our classroom', 'I'm so bummed that I can't stay w/ you next semester', and sent messages like 'is there any way I can take the quiz tomorrow morning at 900 i had an emergency come up I know that I am like in the hole with this class but this is really serious could you please let me know'. In addition to 'w/' for 'with' as seen above, for 'you', 'I', 'by the way', 'because' and 'what', they regularly used unconventional orthography such as 'u', 'i', 'btw', 'b/c' and 'wut', common texting abbreviations.

Some also incorporated the very common 'Ok' as a discourse marker to shift the content of their e-mail back to the main point. For example, this student wrote: 'Hey Dr. [Teacher Name], I just wanted to make sure that it was still ok to come tomorrow during free period to take my exam. I wrote back to you on Friday, but hadn't heard from you so I just wanted to make sure that everything was still set. I also don't know if there is any homework due tomorrow, but if there is could you e-mail it to me? I don't want to be behind on my homework, you know? Ok, so if you could get back to me that would be great. I'll talk to you soon. Thanks!' This use of the informal 'Ok' has an almost oral quality to it, a word one might use as a filler while leaving a voicemail.

Faculty members often react to all of the issues highlighted in this section. Because of aggressive, disrespectful messages and informal language or due to what may be more innocuous features such as typos, abbreviations, or emoticons, teachers can and do react negatively to students' e-mail, sometimes even taking offense. But, as evidenced in this study, the realization that, some, or even many, students do indeed acknowledge norms of e-mail etiquette, along with teachers' more sensitive understanding of the potential reasons behind students' etiquette violations, may help bridge the relational gap between student e-mail senders and faculty recipients. The e-mail setting is indeed challenging for it is often the means by which students must carry out complex, and in some cases face-threatening, pragmatic functions, making requests about course assignments, giving excuses about attendance, complaining about their grades, sending assignments, and expressing gratitude while they simultaneously attempt to develop and maintain the student-teacher relationship.

Students' Actual Use of E-mail: A Summary

Students' beliefs are indeed complex and sometimes difficult to determine but their actual use of e-mail suggests a certain degree of consistency between their beliefs and practices. This section provides an overall report on these data but corresponding topics are explored more fully in subsequent chapters. Overall, the analysis of these messages revealed the following: 828 requests; 250 excuses; 68 thank yous, 17 apologies, and 19 complaints. In addition, 78 messages were coded as 'dropbox'; often these messages also contained requests, excuses, thank yous, etc., an issue to be addressed in Chapter Four (see Table 3.1). However, students also sent e-mails that did not relate to any of the above categories. They included well-wishes when the professor was ill, confirmation of having received a document, or responses to a question asked by their teacher. These 155 messages were coded as 'other'. Finally, students also composed 63 e-mails entirely in Spanish. These were analyzed separately. Because many e-mails were written for more than one purpose, a given message could be coded as an excuse and as a request, or as a thank you and an excuse, and so on; that is, except for 'dropbox', 'other' and 'Only Spanish', the categories were not mutually exclusive.

Table 3.1: Students' E-mail Uses

Requests	Excuses	Thank Yous	Apologies	Complaints	Dropbox	Other	Only Spanish
828	250	68	17	19	78	155	63

Requests

The 828 requests were identified as either requests for information (e.g., 'could you please tell me if we should do both "A" and "B" on p. 135 for homework?;' or, 'does this sentence require an indicative or subjunctive verb?') or for some kind of permission or action on the part of the teacher (e.g., 'would it be okay if I take the quiz in your office tomorrow?;' or, 'would you be willing to write me a letter of recommendation for medical school?'). Multiple requests of the same type sent in one e-mail were counted as one and if a message contained more than one type of request, the message was coded only once depending on its primary request topic. The student's primary request topic was determined by examining either what constituted the largest portion of the message or what topic the e-mail author presented first chronologically, whichever seemed the most likely motivation for the e-mail. As mentioned previously, sometimes request messages included an expression of gratitude; these 695 messages with a 'thank yous' were counted separately from the 68 messages that were coded as authentic thank you e-mails (see Table 3.2). Moreover, some students included only one expression of gratitude in an e-mail while others used multiple 'thank yous', a topic explored in detail in Chapter 5.

Table 3.2: Students' E-mail Requests

	E-mails Including at least 1 *thank you*	E-mails Excluding a *thank you*
Totals	695	133
	828	

Repair Work: Excuses and Apologies

Students' e-mails also contained 267 messages that were categorized as 'repair work'; these included 250 'excuse accounts' and 17 apologies. The majority of the excuses were about a student missing class (197); others related to a student submitting an assignment late, or not at all, as well as to various other situations (53). About 72% of the excuses (179/250) included a specific offer of repair (see Table 3.3). For example, one student explained the reason for her absence and assured the teacher that she would obtain lecture notes from a classmate; another student explained that he had not handed in the homework in class because of a printer problem and offered to drop it off in the professor's office.

Table 3.3: Students' E-mail Excuses

	Excuses Including an Offer of Repair	Excuses Without an Offer of Repair
Totals	179	71
	250	

The data also contained 17 e-mail apologies. These apologies were of a more intentional nature than statements such as 'Sorry for the inconvenience' or 'Sorry to bother you but...' that often accompanied requests. Those kinds of statements, which usually served to soften other speech acts, were not included in the apology category. Counted apologies included those focused on situations such as misunderstandings, missed appointments or concerns over having performed at a level students believed was unacceptable for them. Like their excuse e-mails, students' apology messages sometimes contained offers of repair (see Table 3.4).

Table 3.4: Students' E-mail Apologies

	Apologies Including a Specific Offer of Repair	Apologies Without an Offer of Repair
Totals	10	7
	17	

Thank Yous

Students' 68 thank you e-mails expressed students' gratitude for various actions that had been performed by the teacher: providing registration or advising help, sending a document or homework assignment via e-mail, writing letters of recommendation, answering questions about course material or giving permission for a student to miss class for a special event (see Table 3.5 for a complete account).

Table 3.5: Students' E-mail Thank Yous

Reason for Thank You	Number of E-mails
Providing Registration or Advising Help	13
Sending Homework Assignment or Document	9
Writing a Letter of Recommendation	9
Giving Overall Support as Teacher/Advisor	7
Providing Course Material Help	7
Other/Undeterminable	7
Allowing Rescheduling of an Appointment, Exam, Quiz or Presentation	6
Postponing an Exam, Quiz or Assignment	5
Answering a Grade Question	2
Notifying Student of a Lost Item	2
Granting Permission for a Student to Miss Class for a Special Event	1

Complaints

Student complaint e-mails were very rare. Only 19 were identified in the analysis (see Table 3.6). Other messages contained statements that were complaint-like in nature but they were framed as other functions, usually as requests or excuses. For instance, a request for more information about one's grade sometimes implied a complaint about the way the assessment process had been carried out. Such examples are further analyzed in the chapter on complaints.

Table 3.6: Students' E-mail Complaints

	Number of E-mail Complaints
Grade-Related	17
Teacher's Refusal to Write a Letter of Recommendation	1
Quantity of Work Due on Same Day	1

'Dropbox', 'Only Spanish' and 'Other'

Students' e-mails that were coded 'dropbox' or 'only Spanish' are analyzed in detail in those respective chapters. Messages categorized as 'other' were excluded from further analysis.

Speech Act Combinations

As noted earlier, many messages included more than one speech act or function. Some particularly common combinations were excuse/request (140), complaint/request (17), and apology/request (5). Table 3.7 presents detailed information about these e-mails.

Table 3.7: Students' E-mail Combinations

Types of E-mail Combination	# of E-mails
Excuse with Repair/Request for Information	28
Excuse with Repair/Request for Non-Information	14
Excuse with Repair/Both Request Types	3
Excuse without Repair/Request for Information	61
Excuse without Repair/Request for Non-Information	29
Excuse without Repair/Both Request Types	4
Excuse without Repair/Request for Information/Thank You	1
Complaint/Request for Information	12
Complaint/Request for Non-Information	5
Apology with Repair/Request for Information	2
Apology with Repair/Request for Non-Information	3
Apology without Repair/Request for Information	0
Apology without Repair/Request for Non-Information	0
Thank you/Excuse	3
Thank you/Request	1

Like requests that often contained an expression of gratitude, excuses often contained some expression of apology; but, these apologetic statements were considered an integral part of the excuse rather than as separate apologies. Therefore, that combination was not identified.

The various types of combinations highlighted in Table 3.7 were also found in students' 78 'dropbox' e-mails. Given the distinct nature of these kinds of e-mails, usually containing attached or copy/pasted assignments, they were analyzed separately and are explored in Chapter 4. In addition to providing a better understanding of students' use of e-mail to make requests, offer excuses, express gratitude, apologize and complain, this analysis will shed further light on students' beliefs regarding student-teacher e-mail communication.

CHAPTER FOUR

Students' Use of the Dropbox

'Here it is. You asked me to redo it so i did and decided to email it too you.. thanks.. [Student Name]'

'here you go, im sorry I didn't have it in class today'

'Hey, Dr. [Teacher Name], I ran out of paper so I have to email this to you until I can get some more. It's just proof that I did it on time.'

'Dear Professor: I ran out of ink. Thank you. [Student Name].'

'I tried printing out my papers before class, but it didn't work.. I wil bring a hard copy to you later today. Thank you [Student Name].'

Dropbox Behaviors

Students' use of e-mail as a kind of asynchronous electronic dropbox has been previously studied though not in great detail or with a large database. The term 'asynchronous,' as clarified by Hannah, Glowacki-Dudka, & Conceicao-Runlee (2000: 17), is particularly relevant to the present analysis: 'Synchronous interactions are those in which learners are online at the same time. Asynchronous interactions are those that do not take place in real time. Learners participate in asynchronous course activities at times convenient to them.' Students' use of e-mail to submit course assignments falls neatly into the asynchronous category for students often choose this electronic medium for submitting their work when an assignment is late, the student was or will be absent, or the teacher was or is unavailable, i.e., at a time convenient for the students. Worrells (2001) evaluated the use of e-mail for transmitting information to students and for sending assignments to teachers. In 2001, this use of technology was still relatively novel and students had to be encouraged, or even required, to send e-mail attachments and to learn how to use computers for this purpose. Worrells (2001) found several issues to be problematic for students: their lack of familiarity with attachments; their lack of access to *Microsoft Word*; various problems with file extensions; their preference for submitting assignments in e-mail messages rather than by attachment; and their failure to identify appropriately the assignment they were submitting. But, Worrells (2001) concluded, 'The use of e-mail for coursework has proven to be beneficial to students and this instructor. The advantages to the process far outweigh the disadvantages' (6).

Times have certainly changed. No longer do students need to be encouraged or required to use e-mail for submitting assignments. In fact, many teachers now discourage (and some even prohibit) students from using e-mail at all. For instance, Weiss & Hanson-Baldauf's (2008) research included this teacher's statement regarding e-mail behavior: 'I would like students to ask themselves if the question can wait until my next office hours. I'm simply too busy to reply to all of the e-mails I get from students.' Another report quotes a senior professor who stated, 'I just don't allow e-mail. They can come to office hours if they want' (Mason, 2010). Though the second teacher's approach reportedly prompted a gasp from the other faculty present for the discussion, it is true that there is a growing resentment of e-mail among teachers due to the many hours it forces them to spend online. In addition to the large number of e-mails they manage, faculty members find it time- and resource-consuming to receive student work by attachment, open and print it, and keep up with the accompanying requests for confirmation: 'Did you get my paper?' and 'Would you please confirm that you were able to open the document?'. Nevertheless, e-mail remains a popular medium for students to submit coursework. For various reasons highlighted below, sometimes students even seem to prefer e-mail over other more traditional ways of submitting assignments.

In the present study many students attached documents of various kinds to their messages. These e-mails were not all coded as 'dropbox'; rather, this designation was restricted to messages whose primary purpose was the submission of a document (often attached electronically as a *Microsoft Word* document or copy/pasted in the body of the e-mail) to the teacher. Sometimes students' accompanying messages communicated excuses, requests, apologies, and expressions of gratitude (or combinations thereof), but the principal motivation of these e-mails was simply the successful transmission of their documents. Other messages also coded as 'dropbox' were those in which students sought to confirm that the teacher had already received, either electronically or physically, a student's previously submitted document.

The students in the present study sent 78 'dropbox' messages. Further analysis of these e-mails highlighted specific characteristics that will receive attention in the remainder of this chapter; these include forms of address and openings; pre-closings and closings; opening/closing combinations; subject lines; and pragmatic functions.

Forms of Address and Openings

The category of dropbox e-mails was a particularly interesting data subset in which to explore students' forms of address. Given the specific purpose of these e-mails (i.e., to 'drop off' an assignment or to confirm the teacher had received it), it seemed more likely in this context than in others that students would ignore formal conventions such as salutations, greetings or closings, typically found in more communicative messages; furthermore, it also seemed likely that students would perceive the role of these e-mails to be merely a sort of electronic 'teacher's helper', a function that, from their perspective, might not require the inclusion of pragmatic niceties.

In her study, Economidou-Kogetsidis (2011) explored pragmatic failure in 200 e-mails from non-native English speakers (Greek Cypriot university students). She found that some e-mails were perceived by teachers as impolite due, in part, to students' omission of greetings and closings or to inappropriate or unacceptable forms of address. Though her study did not compare these e-mails with those from native English-speaking students, her findings are important, especially given the scarcity of investigations on related topics. Another study (Bjørge, 2007), whose findings were grounded in Hofstede's (2001) cultural dimension of power distance, highlighted 'considerable variation when it comes to the choice of greeting and complementary close in students' e-mails' (76). Finally, Marques (2008) found 'Cara professora' ('Dear Professor') to be the most common salutation (30.5%) in her data collected from 210 e-mails written by undergraduate students who were speakers of Portuguese.

Even though the cultural and linguistic contexts were very different, it was valuable to compare the present dropbox data with those of Economidou-Kogetsidis (2011). Her findings included ratings from 24 British lecturers who evaluated the students' e-mails, finding some to be impolite or abrupt. The e-mails analyzed in her study were not dropbox e-mails but rather requests for information or for action on the part of the teacher. Specifically, she found that 37% of the 200 e-mails sent by students included the word 'Dear' to start the messages; 31% omitted 'Dear' but included some kind of title and some form of the teacher's name; 14.5% of these e-mails contained a greeting like 'Hi' or 'Hello' along with some form of the professor's name; and 14.5% of these e-mails did not include any form of address (e.g., 'Dear') or any variation of the professor's name. Closely examining the students' accompanying requests, she concluded that 'writing e-mails to authority figures appropriately remains a demanding task' (3209), and even more so for non-native speakers.

A comparison of her results with the findings of the present study raised some questions since the analysis of the present 78 dropbox e-mails produced quite different results in three of the categories (see Table 4.1 for a comparison). Specifically, this analysis found differences of 27% and 25.5%, respectively, between the studies compared in the categories of 'Inclusion of "Dear"' and 'No Form of Address'; moreover, an analysis of the present data support the creation of a new category, 'Greeting Only'.

Table 4.1: Dropbox: Forms of Address/Openings Comparison

	# of e-mails in Economidou-Kogetsidis (2011)	# of e-mails in present study	percentage difference between the two studies
Inclusion of 'Dear'	74 (37%)	8 (10%)	27%
Inclusion of Title and Professor's Name	62 (31%)	17 (22%)	9%
Greeting With Title and Professor's Name	29 (14.5%)	12 (15%)	.5%
No Form of Address	29 (14.5%)	31 (40%)	25.5%
Greeting Only	–	9 (12%)	–
Other	6 (3%)	1 (1%)	2%

In the present study, the final two categories together account for 13% of e-mails and included a total of ten messages: nine messages (12%) that opened with a greeting only ('Hi' or 'Hello'), a category absent in Economidou-Kogetsidis' (2011) data, and one message (1%) that opened with 'Sorry, Professor', placed in the category 'Other'. As a side note, the 21 total greetings (nine in 'Other' and 12 in the 'Greeting with Title and Professor's Name' categories) included 18 instances of 'Hi' or 'Hello' and three instances of 'Hey'.

In addition to establishing a new 'Greeting Only' category, the present study found statistically significant differences in two of the shared categories (calculated with a two-tailed p = value of < 0.0001 and a 99% CI): 'Inclusion of "Dear"' and 'No Form of Address'. Economidou-Kogetsidis' (2011) students included 'Dear' in more e-mails while the present students began more messages without including a form of address. These differences might be explained by the broader range of content (i.e., requests for information and action) and, consequently, a need for more language in Economidou-Kogetsidis (2011), in contrast with the primary purpose of dropbox e-mails which is simply the submission of an assignment. It is also possible that the request e-mails included in Economidou-Kogetsidis (2011) carried higher stakes and were of more potential social risk to the senders, therefore, encouraging more polite speech than necessary in the dropbox e-mails. Certainly, it is also possible that these differences are related to the non-native/native speaker status of the students in each of the studies; on the one hand, native speakers can likely draw on a wider range of vocabulary and syntax than their non-native-speaking counterparts, but on the other, they might not be as careful when writing e-mails due to their possibly higher level of familiarity with this informal writing context or to their higher level of confidence communicating in English.

Preclosings and Closings

Likewise, other significant differences were found when comparing the preclosings and closings students used in both of these studies. Economidou-Kogetsidis (2011) interpreted 'thanks' not as a closing but as a type of message preclosing, and counted only words like 'best' or 'sincerely' as closings. For purposes of comparison, the present study applied the same category restrictions.

As Table 4.2 presents, Economidou-Kogetsidis (2011) found the preclosing use of 'thanks' to occur in 70% of the messages while it occurred in only 50% of the present study's e-mails; additionally, she found that only 23% of the students' e-mails were closed with words such as 'best' or 'sincerely' but in the present data, only 4% of e-mails included these types of sign-offs. Also, in her data, 77% of the messages did not include a closing as compared to 96% of e-mails that did not include a closing in these data (all three findings are statistically significant when calculated with two-tailed p = values of 0.0022, < 0.0001, and < 0.0001, respectively, and a 99% CI).

Table 4.2: Dropbox: Preclosings and Closings Comparison

	# of e-mails in Economidou-Kogetsidis (2011)	# of e-mails in present study	percentage difference between the two studies
Preclosing	140 (70%)	39 (50%)	20%
Closing	45 (23%)	3 (4%)	19%
No Closing	155 (77%)	75 (96%)	19%

In addition, these data revealed more variation in closing strategies on the part of the students in the present study (see Table 4.3). For example, in the 39 messages that included 'thanks' as a preclosing, 30 simply included 'thanks' or 'thank you' but an additional nine messages included a combination sign-off such as 'Thanks, see you later', 'Thank you. See you in class' or 'Have a nice weekend! Thanks.'. In the originally categorized 'No Closing' data (96%), there was evidence of additional closing language that was not recognized in Economidou-Kogetsidis' (2011) study. In the present investigation, for example, 13 messages used informal phrases ('See you later', 'Have a nice weekend!', etc.) as primary sign-offs; four incorporated a form of 'sorry' or 'sorry this is late' to close the message; six simply ended the message with the student's name; three used a traditional closing ('sincerely', etc.); and only 13 did not include any kind of closing or the student's name.

Table 4.3: Dropbox: An Overall Summary of Preclosings and Closings

Thanks	Thanks With Sign-Off Combo	Sign-Off	Sorry	Student Name Only	Closing	No Closing
30 (38%)	9 (12%)	13 (17%)	4 (5%)	6 (8%)	3 (4%)	13 (17%*)

(*percentages do not total 100% due to rounding)

These data suggest that native speakers again have access to a broader repertoire of lexical choices to close messages and that the sign-off 'thanks' should be reexamined as a type of closing. Interestingly, one of the lecturer participants in Economidou-Kogetsidis (2011: 3208) claimed that 'the expression "thank you in advance" demands compliance' and therefore may result in a negative effect on the recipient. Though that research did not recognize 'thank you' as a closing, or even necessarily as a polite preclosing, this phrase (or variations of it) was even found in dropbox e-mails that were not making requests. That is, the students in the present study did not expect the teacher to comply with any demand and usually made no requests of any kind in their dropbox messages; nevertheless, they frequently used this phrase in place of the more traditional and formal 'sincerely', or the like. In contrast to Economidou-Kogetsidis (2011), the present study did not take into account evaluations from a group of teachers; but, it is possible that many teachers, perhaps especially American teachers, would now interpret 'thanks' differently as it may be gaining popularity as a polite closing in its own right. In addition, many students included various other sign-offs such as 'have a nice break' or an expression of apology, phrases that might now be (re)evaluated as polite closings. Six students ended their messages with their name alone (which, though not high on a politeness scale, is a step up from simply ending an e-mail by completing its content), and only 13 messages failed to include any attempt to close the e-mails; it should also be noted that five of these 13 'No Closing' e-mails did not include any text at all and were sent only to transmit the attached document. In sum, if one accepts 'thanks', the other sign-offs, and the six instances of the student's name as polite closings, the large majority of these students' e-mails were closed politely and only 13/78 (17% rather than the previously categorized 96%) of their dropbox e-mails lacked a closing.

Opening/Closing Combinations

Also interesting were these students' opening/closing combinations (see Table 4.4) in their dropbox e-mails. Many students were careful to open and close their messages in some polite manner while others started well but ended abruptly, or vice versa. Others failed pragmatically at both ends.

Table 4.4: Dropbox: Opening/Closing Combinations

	Form of Address And Student Name	No Form of Address, With Student Name	Form of Address, No Student Name	No Form of Address, No Student Name
# of e-mails	34 (44%)	24 (31%)	4 (5%)	16 (21%*)

(*percentages do not total 100% due to rounding)

Thirty-four of these messages (44%) included both a form of address (with or without a 'Dear') along with at least the student's name to close the message (with or without a 'thanks' or other kind of sign-off). Twenty-four e-mails (31%) did not contain any form of address but did include at least the student's name at the end. Four e-mails (5%) did include a form of address but not the student's name. Finally, 16 e-mails (21%) included neither a form of address nor the student's name (some of these did include a 'hello' or a 'hi', however). Of these 16 e-mails, five did not contain any message at all; they were used only to transmit an attached document, and students presumably assumed that the teacher would identify them by their e-mail address or their name typed on the assignment itself. Though students are often criticized for not including forms of address or signing their messages (Stephens, Houser & Cowan, 2009), it is worth noting that 44% of these e-mails had some form of polite opening or closing, 36% included one or the other and only 21% included neither a form of address or the student's name (though some of these did include a closing such as 'Thanks'). This is a particularly interesting finding in the context of dropbox e-mails, a unique use of electronic communication that often seems more related to the successful submission of a document than to interpersonal communication.

Subject Lines

Rife (2007) complained of having received student e-mails lacking subject lines or including subject lines on which was written the entire e-mail message. This complaint could be highly relevant for dropbox e-mails since students may send these messages for primarily functional and practical, rather than communicative, purposes. But, this analysis found that the large majority of these students composed informative subject lines as part of dropbox messages; only one student's e-mail lacked a subject line and included no identification in the message itself of the specific nature of the document that had been attached (see Table 4.5). The content of these e-mails' subject lines ranged from the identification of the attached assignment (e.g., homework, final paper, p. 61 A & B, etc.) to the student's name or course title/number.

Table 4.5: Dropbox: Subject Lines

Assignment in Subject Line	Student Name or Course in Subject Line	Other Identifying Subject Line	No Subject Line, With Identification	No Subject Line, Without Identification
57 (73%)	7 (9%)	2 (3%)	11 (14%)	1 (1%)

The large majority of these e-mails (73%) were sent with explicit subject line labels that clearly identified the primary reason for the message (i.e., a submitted assignment). Another 12% were sent with a student's name, course number or other helpful designation identified in the subject line and in the attached document. Thus, a total of 85% of these dropbox e-mails included informative subject lines. Only 15% of these messages lacked subject lines and most of these messages (14% of the total e-mails) clearly identified the attachment in the body of the message itself. Only one of these e-mails lacked both a subject line and a statement of explanation. Thus, these data do not substantiate this common teacher complaint; to the contrary, they point to a common practice on the part of these students to specify in the subject line the purpose or topic of a message.

Dropbox Pragmatic Functions: Expressions of Gratitude, Apologies, Requests and Excuses

Along with submitting documents or requesting confirmation of the teacher's receipt of their assignments, students used dropbox e-mails to perform other, sometimes related, functions. For example, as mentioned previously, students often closed messages with 'thanks'; others also expressed gratitude (for the opportunity to submit an assignment, for a 'good semester', for the teacher's help, etc.) in the body of their messages. Altogether, 43 dropbox e-mails included some expression of gratitude. Other dropbox messages (23) included apologies (for not handing in an assignment on time or at all, for not being in class, etc.); several (9) made requests (often for confirmation of receiving the document) and a handful (7) provided excuses (for absences or late work); (see Table 4.6).

Table 4.6: Dropbox: Pragmatic Functions

Expressions of Gratitude	Apologies	Requests	Excuses
43	23	9	7

Below are sample e-mails for each of these situations. For instance, thanking the teacher for allowing the electronic submission of the document or accepting the late assignment for a grade relates to the attached documents (sample one); also relevant was apologizing for not having turned in a paper in class and sending it by e-mail (sample two); making an excuse for not having handed in an assignment and attaching it (sample three) or making an excuse for an absence (sample four) connects directly with the reason for the dropbox e-mail (i.e, the attached assignment). Even a request that the teacher confirm receipt of the assignment, by attachment, via her physical mailbox or through a secretary or other teacher, relates to the dropbox nature of the e-mail (sample five).

Sample One: An expression of gratitude
'Dear Dr. [Teacher Name], Thank you again for the extension on this final paper and for not deducting from my grade for the lecture. Both are greatly appreciated. Attached is my third observation paper. Thank you very much for a great, though challenging, semester. Warmly, [Student Name]'

Sample Two: An apology
'Hi Dr. [Teacher Name], I apologize for not having this in class, because I hadn't purchased the packet yet. Also, somehow I must have missed the folder going around to collect the exercises, because I still had mine in my

folder. I hope that the email will suffice this time. Thanks so much – see you Thursday, [Student Name].'

Sample Three: An excuse (not handing in an assignment)
'Hello, I am at home and I had asked someone if they could hand in my paper for me. However, I have been trying to reach them for the past hour or more to no avail, and I am just getting a little worried. They may have handed in the paper, but if they slept in or something and haven't, I want to at least e-mail the attached files to you. I apologize for this inconvenience, and understand that it was my responsibility to make sure my work got handed in. Respectfully, [Student Name]

P.S. Happy Holidays! And thanks for another enjoyable semester.'

Sample Four: An excuse (an absence)
'[Teacher Name], Since I was out sick the last time we had class I didn't have the opportunity to turn in the last resumen [summary] assignment. I tried stopping by your office once or twice but you weren't there so I thought I should send it to you before the last class before spring break so I've attached the file. See you in class, [Student Name]'

Sample Five: A request
'Dr. [Teacher Name], it turned out that i didnt need the online sources. i hope that the conference went well. by the way, the theology secratary dropped off my paper for me since she was headed upstairs when she gave out our exams. let me know if you got it please. i forgot to check on my way out. thanks for a great semester. [Student Name]'

Sample Five provides evidence that unless students hand in assignments through traditional, routine means (i.e., passing papers to the front of the class or placing them directly in a teacher's homework folder), they sometimes worry that the teacher might not have received them. Another example is a student who had left his paper with a different professor to give to the teacher: 'If you see [the other teacher], could you just send me a quick email saying that you have received [my assignment]?'. Another explained, 'I am just writing to make sure you got my final paper. I slid it under your door, but just in case I am attaching a copy to this email too'. Finally, another e-mailed, 'I'm writing to let you know that I dropped off my final investigative project in your mailbox at about 8:35 a.m. today, Wednesday, May 2 because I had a final at 9 a.m. and could not make it to your office at 10 a.m. Please let me know if for some reason you did not get my paper, and I will e-mail it to you.' Students used dropbox e-mails to document their efforts and ensure that the teacher had successfully received their assignments.

There is also evidence in these data that, despite many significant improvements in technology and e-mail performance, students' insecurities regarding technology's performance (Crouch & Montecino, 1997) remain today. For example, students' e-mails included requests such as 'If you could let me know that you got it that would be great', 'If you have any problems opening it let me know', 'Please let me know if you dont get it' and 'if you could would you mind sending me an e-mail telling me that you received it. If you are having trouble with it I can bring you a hard copy tomorrow'. In all of these cases, 'it' refers to their attached documents.

Rarely (nine messages) did students include any requests in their dropbox e-mails, especially requests unrelated to the attached document. Here are two exceptions:

> **Exception One:**
> 'Hello! Thank you so much for ... I am attaching my study guide- hopefully it works ... and if you get a spare moment, would you mind very much to send my current grade? Thank you so much! [Student Name]'

This student's e-mail illustrates well the multiple purposes for which students send messages, even those primarily intended for the dropbox. She opened her message with a thank you unrelated to her attached study guide and then used the dropbox feature of e-mail to send her assignment to the teacher. Finally, she made a request, separate from both her expression of gratitude and her submitted assignment, and closed her message with another thank you that seems related to her request and her hope that the teacher will comply. This 'Thank you so much' is of the variety that was interpreted negatively by some teachers (Economidou-Kogetsidis, 2011). However, this student's softeners, 'if you get a spare minute' and 'would you mind very much', attempted to counter the expectation of compliance that her 'thank you' might imply.

Another message was similar to Exception One in that it also was aimed at more than one purpose and included a final, possibly problematic, 'thank you':

> **Exception Two:**
> 'Dr. [Teacher Name], I put my final paper in your drop box since you were not in your office. I hope it is still there when you get there. Anyway I am sending you an electronic copy as well just in case. Also thanks for a great semester, this was a challenging yet very enjoyable class. My minor has still not come up on my cirriculum tracking program online and I was wondering if the registrar has contacted you or not. Thanks again and have a great summer. [Student Name]'

In addition to using e-mail's dropbox feature and submitting an additional electronic copy 'just in case', this student also expressed gratitude for a 'great semester'. He then asked the teacher, who also was one of his academic advisors, a question about his minor, a request unrelated to the attached document but closely related to his status as a graduating senior. His message closed with a combination sign-off, 'Thanks again and have a great summer', an expression of gratitude seemingly related to his advising request for information. The phrasing of his particular request does not entail significant effort on the part of the instructor who could simply answer, affirmatively or negatively, if she had been contacted by the registrar about his situation. However, since he was graduating in about a week, the student's request was more involved than its phrasing suggests and required that the teacher follow up on his situation with the appropriate administrative office. His 'Thanks again' was more likely related to this recognized though unspoken request; his indirect approach could be taken by some to be polite, though others might view his manner of asking for help as convoluted or confusing, and, in turn, his 'Thanks' as insincere or even demanding. But, familiarity with a particular student can go a long way toward easily accepting such a message and complying with the request in good will.

Another student's dropbox email, this time an apology, might also produce a negative effect but for a slightly different reason. He wrote,

> 'Dr. [Teacher Name], I'm so sorry that I did not have the paper in to you by 10 this morning. It is almost two at the moment and I am dropping it off to you in your box. I am also going to email it to you [it was attached]. Sorry about this. Thank you for a very enjoyable semester ... i learned a lot. [Student Name]
> Thanks again enjoy the summer'

Though he submitted his assignment late and with an apology, his e-mail did not include even a hint of recognition that the teacher might not accept his final paper, an omission that could cause annoyance or even rejection on the part of a teacher. However, he did specifically acknowledge the lateness of his work, submitted his assignment both physically in the teacher's mailbox as well as electronically in her inbox, thanked her for an enjoyable semester, claimed to have benefited from the class and signed his name (without any kind of traditional closing). Interestingly, as if he realized that he had failed to end his message as politely as possible, he then wrote an additional statement, placing it under his name, that included a combination 'thanks again'/'enjoy the summer' sign-off. Though he failed to articulate that his teacher might not accept the attached document, his apology, dropbox actions, expressions of gratitude and summer well-wishes together attempted to mitigate the situation.

Despite the lack of explicit recognition in those e-mails, many students submitting late or missing assignments did explicitly acknowledge that the teacher might not accept them and used language that corresponded to this reality. For instance, one student offered an excuse as to why she hadn't handed in an assignment and left it up to the teacher to accept or reject her late work:

> 'Hello Dr. [Teacher Name], I'm not sure if the folder never came around to me in class last Thursday, or if I just missed it, but I only realized this afternoon that I still have my essay in my Linguistics folder; somehow I didn't turn it in in class. I attached it to this email, *even though* I realize that it is probably considered late at this point. I will also bring both the rough draft and final copies to class tomorrow, if you'd still accept them. Thanks See you on Monday, [Student Name]' (italics added for emphasis)

Despite attaching her work, the student's use of 'even though' expressed her understanding that it was now 'late'; moreover, she also promised to bring additional hardcopies to class if the teacher was willing to accept them. Other students in similar situations included phrases such as 'Hope that's okay' and 'Hope this doesn't cause any inconvenience' to attempt to communicate understanding of their imposition.

Similar to Sample Four above, several students recognized that dropbox e-mails could be used as 'proof' that an assignment had been completed on time. Some even explicitly acknowledged that this was the purpose of their e-mail. They made statements such as 'I'm emailing you a copy so that you know I did my homework'; 'I ran out of paper so i have to email this to you until i can get some more. It's just proof that i did it on time'; and 'I have attached it to this email, but I will drop off a hard copy tomorrow ... I just wanted to make dure that you knew i did it'.

As has already been documented above, the practice of submitting both hard and electronic copies of the same assignment was very popular. Many students who sent an attached document either promised to bring a hard copy to the next class, said they had already dropped off a hard copy in the teacher's mailbox or offered to submit an assignment in hard copy as well, if the teacher so desired. Finally, the students' language reflected the dropbox nature of these e-mails; many explained in the body of their message what was attached and 24 of their messages included specific 'here-phrases' such as 'here is', 'here are', 'here it is' and 'here you go' as well as 'I have attached...'.

Pedagogical Implications and Future Research

The particular pragmatic functions (apologies, requests, etc.) introduced in this section on dropbox e-mails will be explored in greater detail in subsequent chapters. However, several important pedagogical implications have already surfaced and will be highlighted below. This analysis of dropbox e-mails also points to several areas for future research directly related to this particular use of e-mail by students. Of course, this is not meant to be an exhaustive list but its aim is to provide teachers and researchers with questions and issues to reflect on and explore as desired.

First, based on dropbox messages as well as on students' general e-mail use, future research should more thoroughly investigate teachers' preferences for particular forms of address, openings and closings. Since these lexical choices have the capacity to provoke negative reactions from teacher recipients as well as carry relational and sometimes academic consequences, future investigations should better establish the range of teachers' expectations regarding these e-mail issues. In the meantime, since teachers' perspectives are as yet undocumented, students should be given some leeway in making choices and trying to find their own way to achieve successful, polite communication with their teachers on e-mail.

Second, more studies should be carried out to investigate students' use of particular forms of address, openings and closings. Larger sample sizes and highly detailed analyses would go a long way toward the development of a better understanding of their current practices in various settings (different academic disciplines, native/non-native speaking students, multiple languages used in e-mails, etc.) and, in turn, more productive teaching strategies to foster better student e-mail etiquette.

Third, research should focus on distinguishing the different characteristics of dropbox e-mails and e-mails used for other communicative purposes (making a request, apologizing, etc.). Given the varying levels of risk involved in writing different types of e-mails to teachers, it is likely that important distinctions will emerge.

Fourth, the present data pointed to the possible need to reevaluate students' use of 'thanks' as a polite closing. Moreover, future studies should also specifically explore the popularity and effects of other potentially polite closings such as 'see you in class' and 'sorry' as well as e-mails that close with only the student's name or nothing at all. Given the fact that some faculty complain about the quantity and length of e-mails they receive, students are in the complex situation of needing to compose concise messages without needless words while still maintaining lexical features that create a polite impression on teachers. This may be especially relevant in the dropbox e-mail context. Again, especially until more is known about students' current practices and teachers' actual preferences, students' attempts to use polite markers, even those that are not among the 'traditionally preferred', should not be overlooked.

Fifth, despite the dropbox purpose of these e-mails, since this analysis found that 44% of these messages included some form of opening/closing combination and 73% included informative subject lines, educators should ask themselves why some teachers criticize students so frequently for not attempting to send polite e-mails or for sending e-mails that lack necessary information. Is it possible that teachers' reactions are based on the relatively few impolite or confusing e-mails they receive? Is it also possible that the complaint about their lacking subject lines is motivated by faculty's desire to more easily access past e-mails through the use of informative labels? Indeed, do teachers even read most subject lines before they read the students' messages? Do they ever read them? These are questions that research probably cannot answer but that teachers might ask themselves as they react, and analyze their reactions, to students' messages. In addition to studying features of students' openings and closings, future investigations could explore how subject lines in dropbox e-mails may vary from those accompanying other types of e-mail communication.

Sixth, this analysis of dropbox e-mails included only 9/78 requests (12%). Compared with the number of requests in the overall e-mail data collected (excluding dropbox e-mails and messages written entirely in Spanish), the frequency of requests was quite different. In the overall data, 832/1,403 (59%) of the e-mails contained a request of some sort. Thus, it seems clear that these students viewed and used dropbox e-mails very differently from other more communicative messages. Future investigations could explore these issues more fully. However, since students did use dropbox e-mails to accomplish more than one purpose (i.e., to submit an assignment and make an excuse; to confirm that the teacher received a document and apologize, etc.), the nature of these 'multi-purpose e-mails' could be compared to that of other e-mails that are not used to submit an assignment.

Seventh, teachers should be sensitive to the fact that students use one message for multiple purposes and, therefore, be careful readers. If teachers do not want to receive additional, follow-up e-mails from students whose purposes were not served by their original messages, they would be wise to address each of the issues which call for a response (i.e., answer the question, respond to the request, and confirm receipt of the attachment when requested, etc.). If a teacher's own understanding of good e-mail etiquette includes the rule that separate messages should be composed to address multiple issues, teachers should communicate that expectation to students. Otherwise, it is in a teacher's best interest (i.e., the teacher will receive fewer follow-up e-mails) to respond in some way to the multiple issues raised by a student in the same e-mail. Moreover, since these data show clear evidence that students worry about the successful transmission of documents, it could be useful for teachers to make it a routine practice to reply to a received attachment with a simple 'Got it'. Even just this brief acknowledgment, taking seconds at most, would confirm that an assignment was successfully received and would foster a mutually respectful working relationship between teacher and student.

Eighth, it would prevent some misunderstandings and negative judgments if teachers would be appropriately open to the ever-changing nature of language and to the new lexical additions that developing technologies bring. These data showed that these students generally tried to be polite. Faculty who are open to accepting, or at least tolerating, common e-mail language characteristics (such as emoticons, informal greetings such as 'Hey', and grammatical deviations) and relatively newer politeness markers (e.g., 'asap', 'thanks', etc.), have a better chance of staying in touch with students and positively influencing their attitudes toward, and use of, language, even on e-mail.

Finally, in terms of e-mail etiquette, not all students seem aware that acknowledging that an assignment is late and therefore might not be accepted is more positively received than a 'Here is my paper – thanks' dropbox e-mail. For teachers willing or desiring to address appropriate e-mail behaviors, this is a topic that could be explored with students so that they can learn to see the potential effects, both positive and negative, their messages might have on teacher recipients. Helping students carry out a thoughtful pragmatic analysis of sample e-mails, combined with instruction about presuppositions, politeness norms, etc., has the side benefit of expanding students' understanding of language and how it functions in a real-life setting. Also, many of these students who submitted assignments by attachment had already provided teachers with hard copies in class or offered to do so later. This practice, since it communicates responsibility and respect, should be encouraged by teachers as a part of e-mail etiquette.

CHAPTER FIVE

Requests

'Hola! I was just wondering if you could tell me what the homework is for tomorrow. I forgot to write it down after the test and I talked to a couple other people and they forgot, too, so I figured I would ask you. Thank you!'

Reflecting on the typical content of their inboxes, most teachers would likely recognize that the most common messages from students communicate some kind of request. As a positive result, this realization might confirm a teacher's sense of usefulness or, more negatively, it could foster annoyance or even impatience on the part of some teachers who tire of receiving fairly consistent requests. Added to the workload these messages create is the offense that some teachers feel when students' requests are expressed in ways that 'sound rude' or 'seem demanding,' common complaints expressed by teachers about student e-mail in general (Hartford & Bardovi-Harlig, 1996; Weinstock, 2004; Glater, 2006; Biesenbach-Lucas, 2007; Stephens, Houser & Cowan, 2009; Economidou-Kogetsidis, 2011; among others).

As previously explained in Chapters 1 and 3, a tremendous amount of research has already been conducted on student e-mail requests, especially if one compares that body of work with the overall number of investigations on other types of student e-mail such as complaints and apologies. (See, for example, Biesenbach-Lucas, 2005; 2006; 2007; Bloch, 2002; Economidou-Kogetsidis, 2011; Glater, 2006; Hartford & Bardovi-Harlig, 1996; Martin, Myers & Mottet, 1999; Samar, Navidinia & Mehrani, 2010.) Thus, rather than duplicate those efforts, the present analysis takes a broader view of these issues as seen through the relatively large set of data currently under analysis.

As emphasized by Biesenbach-Lucas (2006), the application of existing coding categories continues to be a complicated issue. Especially with naturalistic data (i.e., e-mails sent by real people in real-life situations), these coding frameworks require significant revision and the addition of new categories, as well as extensive rater reliability procedures and training, to be meaningful. Without such attention, the results of different studies cannot legitimately be compared. Analyzing complex notions such as directness and politeness across data sets by multiple researchers requires careful attention to category types and coding procedures at a level that is likely impossible to achieve reliability.

In addition, given the relatively large number of request e-mails in the present investigation, it seemed more useful to carry out an analysis that would provide baseline data on which future research might draw. Thus, though it is widely known by both researchers and teachers that students often send request e-mails, this chapter will report on the nature of those requests. That is, what did these students actually request from their teacher? For what practical needs did they choose to communicate with their teacher by e-mail? And how did they express those requests?

Researchers have long noted that Americans often use expressions of gratitude, particularly 'thank you,' in ways that are viewed as mechanical (Apte, 1974). However, ironically, studies have also shown that teachers negatively evaluate students' e-mail requests that lack an expression of gratitude, even a simple 'thank you, [Student Name]', and consider them rude or selfish (Economidou-Kogetsidis, 2011). Thus, it seems that even the somewhat automated use of 'thank you' as a brief e-mail closing is enough to satisfy face-considerations (Brown and Levinson, 1987), positive or negative, for at least some teachers.

Interestingly, Eisenstein and Bodman (1986) claimed that shorter thanking episodes usually reflect 'greater social distance between interlocutors' (176). Specifically, expressions of gratitude among interlocutors of unequal status were usually unelaborated (i.e., shorter, infrequent, less complex vocabulary, less personal) when, in contrast, expressions of gratitude were more elaborated (i.e., longer, more frequent, more complex vocabulary, more personal) among friends. Therefore, it would be expected that brief 'thank yous' would be more common between students and their teacher, a relationship of relatively unequal status.

A cross-cultural study by Lee & Park (2011) compared favor-asking messages written by 224 undergraduate Korean and American students in their respective native languages. This favor-asking e-mail was elicited by asking each student to imagine that he or she, as a small group member of a large lecture class, had been sick. Student participants were asked to e-mail their group mates, whom they had not yet met, 'to let them know that you are very sick and to ask if the meeting can be rescheduled' (131). The experiment instructions and prompt, as well as the students' resulting e-mails, were all composed in the participants' native languages. Lee & Park (2011) found that the Korean students, writing in Korean, included significantly more apologies as part of their favor-asking messages, but the American participants, writing in English, included significantly more expressions of gratitude.

Lee & Park (2011) identified apology phrases as 'I am (really, very, so) sorry,' 'Sorry,' and 'I apologize' in both Korean and English (132). Expressions of gratitude included 'Thanks,' 'I would (really) appreciate,' 'It would be appreciated,' and 'Thank you (very much)' in both languages. They coded each e-mail as an 'Apology,' a 'Thank you,' an example of 'Both,' or of 'None,' depending on the particular content of each message.

Their results reveal statistically significant cultural differences. As part of their favor-asking messages, 105/127 Koreans (82.7%) included one or more apologies as compared to only 51/97 Americans (52.6%). However, interestingly, 12/127 Koreans (9.4%) included one or more expressions of gratitude as compared to 72/97 (74.2%) Americans. Moreover, more Koreans used multiple apologies in the same e-mail than did the Americans but more Americans used multiple expressions of gratitude – in fact, none of the Koreans expressed thank you more than once in the same e-mail. As Lee & Park (2011) noted, the Americans repeated their gratitude while the Koreans repeated their apologies.

The present data provide some interesting points of comparison with Lee & Park (2011). It is important to note, however, that the requests examined here include requests of various types, both information and action-related, unlike the favor-asking request e-mails prompted by one hypothetical situation (Lee & Park 2011). Moreover, the present requests were written by students for their actual teacher, known interlocutors of unequal status, whereas the requests written by the participants in Lee & Park (2011) were designed for hypothetical student peers, interlocutors of more or less equal status.

Additionally, the present naturalistic e-mails were all written for the same teacher who was known by most of the students. That represented a constant in this study ensuring that e-mail authors were all thinking of the same teacher when they composed their messages. Furthermore, though the request contexts varied, they each represented typical student-teacher e-mail request interactions motivated by genuine needs. The present analysis sought to determine if these students followed the pattern found in Lee & Park (2011) of including more expressions of gratitude than apology in this authentic context. It also analyzed the degree to which these students repeated their use of specific politeness strategies, such as expressions of gratitude, apology, and 'please,' in the same message.

Request Topics

As documented in Chapter 3, these students sent 828 e-mails containing a request(s). Many requested that the teacher provide some kind of written information (e.g., the homework assignment, office hour or location details, course advising details, etc.) but others were directed at some other type of response on the part of the teacher (e.g., scheduling a meeting, granting an extension, postponing a presentation, etc). Table 5.1 presents the categories coded in the analysis as well as the number of requests related to each category.

Table 5.1: Request Topics

E-Mail Request Topic	# of e-mails	% of total requests
Advice / Help	454	55%
Request a Meeting	127	15%
Send the Homework Assignment	86	10%
Postponement / Extension / Rescheduling	78	9%
Permission to Enroll in Course	28	3%
Permission to Make Up Exam or Quiz	18	2%
Letter of Recommendation / Serve as Reference	15	2%
Send a Document	13	2%
Change a Grade	9	1%
Totals	828	99% (due to rounding)

The Advice/Help category included a variety of individual topics closely related to common student-teacher interactions; for example, students asked about the date of an exam, for course advising, how to do an assignment, what an upcoming quiz would be like, what an upcoming course would be like, for current course grade information, for help with vocabulary or homework, and so on. Since a teacher's advice often includes specific help (and vice versa), it seemed logical to group these request types into one broad category. Below are two typical examples of such e-mails:

> Dear Professor [Teacher Name],
> I hope you had a wonderful holiday season! Mine was awesome if you were wondering. I just wanted to ask you one quick question. Along with the new stuff ill be learning next semester, i was just wondering if u could quickly tell me one or two things that we covered that i should study again in order to

get a better grade next semester. Like just what my weakest areas were in your class. It would be such a huge help to me. Thanks very much. Enjoy the rest of your break! [Student Name]

if I wanted to say, 'At the same time, a strange man followed me,' would that be preterite or imperfect? i was leaning more toward imperfect, though:) thank you [Student Name]

The second largest category was that of Request a Meeting. Some students explained their limited availability and requested a meeting outside their teacher's regular office hours or they e-mailed their teacher to confirm that it was okay to 'stop by' during her posted hours. For example,

Dr. [Teacher Name],
Is there anyone [sic] we can meet before class tomorrow? I wanted to talk to you about the classes I am taking while in Spain. thank you so much [Student Name]

The third most frequent category contained students' requests that the teacher Send the Homework Assignments. These requests sometimes accompanied absence excuses, sent prior to or following the actual absence. They simultaneously communicated to the teacher that (or why) the student would be/was absent and asked her to send the homework assignment by e-mail.

Hi [Teacher Name],
Sorry to bother you but I was just wondering if you could please give me the next assignment that we have to do for Monday. It would help me out so much because I have a very busy weekend. If you could please get back to me I would appreciate it. Thank you so much for your time and have a great day! Sincerely, [Student Name]

Dr. [Teacher Name],
Im very sorry that I was not in class yesterday but I was throwing up all day and did not think it would be the best thing to sit in class while I was feeling this way. I have the homework that I am caught up on and what was due yesterday and I was hoping you could email me the assignment for thurs. Im very sorry again I did not plan on this. thank you for understanding. [Student Name]

A large number of requests related to students' requests for Extensions on various assignments or Postponement/Rescheduling of papers, presentations, exams, and even class itself on one occasion! (The university had reached the basketball tournament finals and a student requested that the teacher either cancel class completely or at least allow unexcused absences for those who wanted to watch or attend the game.) These requests often included accompanying apologies and/or explanations regarding why the student faced a late work situation, but sometimes they did not. For instance,

> Hi Dr. [Teacher Name]
> *I wanted to let you know that I probably won't have the final handed in by tomorrow at 10. I am going to try my hardest to finish it, but the odds are not good. I was wondering if, in the event that I didn't finish it tonight, I could hand it in on Thursday. I understand that this may cause me to lose some points on my grade. However, I would rather hand in to you something I took time working on, rather than something I just rushed through. Sincerely, [Student Name]*

The remainder of the e-mails together account for about 10% of the total requests and will not be analyzed in further detail.

Common Lexical Items

> Dr. [Teacher Name],
> I was wondering *if you found my notebook on one of the desks during our last classes. I think I left it in that room and when I went back to look for it, it wasn't there. I was just wondering, if you could get back to me I would appreciate it. Thank you. [Student Name]*

As documented by many researchers such as Murphy & Neu (1996) who analyzed e-mails in a complaint context and Biesenbach-Lucas (2006) who studied e-mails in a request context, many particular words and phrases are used frequently by students. Students frequently included particular lexical items to soften or mitigate the imposition of their requests. Four of the most common are included in this analysis (expressions of gratitude, apologies, and 'please' will be addressed in subsequent sections).

It was interesting to note that the most frequent phrase, used in approximately one third of the students' e-mails, was 'I/We was/were (just) wondering...' (see Table 5.2), a common phrase also found in complaint e-mails (Murphy & Neu, 1996). Students incorporated variations of this phrase at the beginning, middle, and end of their e-mails – and sometimes more than once. The mitigator 'just' was also used by many students. The e-mail introducing this section illustrates both of these strategies.

Table 5.2: Lexical Items in Requests

Lexical Item	# of e-mails containing at least one occurrence
'I/We was/were (just) wondering...'	246 (30%)
'just'	211 (26%)
'is/was there any way that...'	23 (3%)
'I was hoping (that) (you)...'	15 (2%)

'Just' was sometimes used as part of 'I was just wondering' but it was also used in the following types of expressions to soften the accompanying request:

> *hey..*just *a request... do u think it would be possible to* just *ballpark my grade like..*just *wether its over a C..*

> *I* just *had a couple of questions*

> *I* just *wanted ...*

The less common phrase 'is/was there any way that ...' was either embedded in declarative sentences such as 'I wanted to know if there was any way that you could grant me an extension' or in questions such as 'Is there any way that you can tell me what the composicion will be on so that maybe I can gather information or start it?'. Though, of course, there usually exists 'a way' to satisfy most students' requests, teachers are often unwilling to do so for a variety of reasons. Many students politely account for this possibility by providing the teacher with an easy 'out', as did the same student whose e-mail concluded: 'That would be such a big help but if you are not able I understand. Thank you soo much for your time.'

Also noteworthy was students' use of 'I was hoping' to frame requests such as 'I was hoping that we could arrange a time to meet tomorrow' or 'I was hoping that you would be willing to consider writing me a letter of recommendation'. As well documented in previous studies, students also frequently used modals and other common phrases such as 'I wanted to know if ...' to communicate their requests, but these were not tracked in the analysis.

Finally, occurring only once but noted here due to its novelty was the phrase 'could you happen to ...'. It was embedded in the following request for grade information: 'Whenever you get a chance could you happen to tell me what my final grade is and what I had gotten on the final..thanks again for everything'. Though semantically impossible since 'happen to' usually implies an accidental action, this phrase was clearly meant to soften the student's request.

Expressions of Gratitude and Apology

Lee & Park's (2011) comparison of English and Korean favor-asking messages focused on expressions of gratitude and apology. Both of these were also coded in the present analysis which recognized related phrases and words such as 'thank you,' 'I (really) appreciate,' and 'I would be grateful if' as expressions of gratitude and '(I am) (really) sorry,' and 'I apologize' as expressions of apology (see Table 5.3). Most student e-mails expressed gratitude and/or apology in an unelaborated (Eisenstein and Bodman, 1986), though appropriate, manner. For example,

Table 5.3: Total Expressions of Gratitude and Apology

	total # of expression	total # of e-mails containing at least one expression	% of total request e-mails
Expressions of Gratitude	813	695	84%
Expressions of Apology	159	135	16%

Dr. [Teacher Name],
My Spanish textbook is missing and i was wondering if i left it in your office on thursday or in the classroom. If you could please let me know. Thanks, [Student Name]

Hi!
I'm really sorry but things got really crazy last week and I couldn't make it to your office. If it's not to late for this year than I'll come in on Thursday around 11:30-11:45 Thanks, [Student Name]

What is most striking is that 695/828 request e-mails (84%) contained at least one expression of gratitude. Compared to 135/828 e-mails (16%) containing at least one apology, this finding is quite noteworthy and confirms Lee & Park's (2011) observation that Americans include more expressions of gratitude than apology with their e-mail requests. However, these students' naturalistic data included expressions of apology much less frequently (in only 16% of the e-mail requests) than did Lee & Park's (2011) American participants (52.6% of their favor-asking messages) who provided elicited data in their experiment setting. Nevertheless, given the very different request types and situational contexts, this comparison should not be exaggerated. What is clear is that the present students used more expressions of gratitude than apologies to accompany their requests.

Lee & Park (2011) also tracked the number of gratitude and apology expressions offered by each individual participant; they found that 18.6% of the Americans included more than one gratitude expression in the same e-mail. But, they found that only 10.3% of Americans included more than one apology expression in the same e-mail. In the present study, these findings were confirmed (see Table 5.4).

Table 5.4: Occurrences of Multiple Expressions of Gratitude and Apology

	# of e-mails	% of total requests	# of e-mails	% of total requests
	Gratitude		Apology	
1 Expression	587	71%	112	14%
2 Expressions	100	12%	22	3%
3 Expressions	7	1%	1	0%
4 Expressions	0	0%	0	0%
5 Expressions	1	0%	0	0%
Total E-Mails Containing at least 1 Expression	695	84%	135	16%

As can be seen above, many students included more than one gratitude expression in the same e-mail (13% total) but few students included more than one apology expression in the same e-mail (3% total). For example, the following student included three expressions of gratitude:

> *Hola. [Hello.] Thank you for your response. If you wouldn't mind though, I would really appreciate it if you could send me the specifics of my grade when you get home from your vacation. Thank you very much, and I hope you enjoyed your vacation. [Student Name]*

Thus, though direct comparisons should not be made, Lee & Park's (2011) overall findings, in regard to their American participants, were confirmed in this much larger, naturalistic data set. These students were much more likely to express gratitude than apologize and more likely to repeat their gratitude than their apologies as part of their request-making e-mails.

Eisenstein and Bodman's (1986) notion of elaborated thanking episodes should again be mentioned here. While it is true that many students did indeed repeat their gratitude, few did so in any way that could be described as truly 'elaborate'. That is, only 13% included multiple expressions of gratitude with their requests and few of them incorporated the kinds of personal expressions that Eisenstein and Bodman (1986) would view as elaborate. That is not to say that these students' expressions of gratitude were not sincere. Rather, their gratitude was expressed politely, and often as part of an opening or closing routine, not as expressions of deep indebtedness or appreciation, expressions which would have been inappropriate given the degree of imposition usually associated with their actual request content. However, it should be noted that students' other messages composed as legitimate thank you e-mails, examined in Chapter 8, did contain characteristics that more closely resemble those highlighted by Eisenstein and Bodman (1986).

Lee & Park (2011) also examined the combination of gratitude and apologies in individual messages. Their American participants more often combined expressions of gratitude and apology (38%) than included either alone (36% and 14%, respectively) or neither (11%). In the present analysis, the results were much different. These students were much less likely to combine expressions of gratitude and apology (only 13%) (see Table 5.5). In fact, they were just as likely to include neither type of expression (13%) as to combine them both. Students were much more likely to include one or more instances of just one or the other (74% total) with their expressions of gratitude (74%) dramatically outnumbering their expressions of apology (3%).

Table 5.5: Combinations of Expressions of Gratitude and Apology

	# of each occurrence (total # of e-mails containing at least one occurrence)	% of total request e-mails
Gratitude	587	71%
Apology	27	3%
Both	107	13%
None	107	13%
Totals	828	100%

Again, statistical comparisons with Lee & Park (2011) would be inappropriate given the numerous and important differences in request type, context, data collection, etc. But, it is of value to note that these students were as likely to include both types of expressions as neither and that their choice of expressions of gratitude far outnumbered those of apology, even though both were used throughout the body of their e-mails as well as to open and close their messages.

'Please'

A final focus of the present analysis was the students' use of 'please' as a politeness marker. Despite the fact that 'please' is presented both to little children as well as adult language learners as a token of politeness to be used when making a request, the students used 'please' in only 19% of these messages (see Table 5.6). Given the varied strategies students used to compose polite messages, it is interesting that the common 'please' was used relatively infrequently. And, when it was used, it was typically used only once in a given e-mail.

Table 5.6: Frequency of 'Please'

	# of e-mails	% of total requests
1 Occurrence	147	18%
2 Occurrences	9	1%
3 Occurrences	1	0%
Total Occurrences of 'please'	157	19%

Alone, these calculations could tempt one to conclude that students' e-mails lacked politeness. But, given the overall findings, it makes more sense to conclude that these students preferred other politeness markers and strategies over the use of 'please' in e-mails to their teacher. In fact, there were several messages without any typical politeness markers that still came across as polite. For example, this message was composed by a student working with a class partner on a presentation:

> *hi, rachel and i are working on our presentation for thursday on the smith article. we were thinking about playing the spanish version of mad gab to demonstrate how students confuse words with each other because they sound similar. i cant find any sites online for spanish mad gab. do you know of anywhere i could find a list of spanish homonyms? i hope you had a good weekend! [Student Name]*

Though the above e-mail lacks any clear expressions of gratitude, apology, or 'please,' and it does not contain any modals or mitigators to accompany the request for help, the message does not come across as rude or impolite. Perhaps the weekend well-wishes at the end serve to soften the request or the students' clear attempt to be diligent and creative in preparing their presentation communicates seriousness rather than flippancy, but it is nevertheless interesting to note that even in the absence of typical politeness markers, this student manages to communicate the request appropriately. Other messages coded as 'None' and lacking 'please' successfully accomplished a similarly polite tone.

There were other messages that may not be interpreted as generously by most teachers. The following two messages also lack politeness markers:

> I can't find the audio files again and I don't know what to do.

> Dear Dr. [Teacher Name],
> I was trying to do the homework tonight and I do not understand the story called Epigrama. It is very confusing, I am not sure what the author is talking about. Also I guess I should just copy all the missing pages in my workbook and then I can do them. So on Thursday after class can i copy the pages that are due Wednesday? Sincerely [Student Name]

In the context of making requests, indirectness is often associated with politeness. Interestingly, the relatively indirect nature of both of these students' requests might actually be negatively interpreted by teachers. The brevity of the first message could come across as terse and, despite the use of a formal greeting and salutation, the rambling nature of the second message might convey a certain degree of irresponsibility on the part of the student.

However, it should be noted that both of these students found themselves in negative homework-related situations. In fact, the subject line of the first message, 'Audio Troubles,' clearly acknowledged that the student was experiencing a problem and her message communicated that she did not know what to do about it. Her use of 'again' reflected that this had happened to her before resulting in frustration about the situation; moreover, her awareness that her grade depended on her successful access to the homework audio files likely prompted a (perhaps) hastily written e-mail lacking common politeness markers. The second message also communicated the student's frustration over not understanding a homework assignment that she deemed 'confusing.' Her wordy description of her situation reflected that she did not know what to do. Further complicating issues was the fact that she was using a textbook that had pages missing. Again, these factors may have led to a less than typical (for her) e-mail. She opened and closed the e-mail in a conventional manner but the body of the message lacked other types of politeness markers.

Pedagogical Implications and Future Research

There are several clear implications for teachers that stem from this analysis of student requests. First, teachers should expect that students will make many requests by e-mail. Indeed, requests were the most common speech act identified in the present analysis. Second, in terms of topic, teachers should anticipate that most student requests will be associated with general academic and course-related situations such as advising issues, homework assignments, meeting requests, assignment details, and so on. Teachers should also expect to find lexical items typically associated with politeness including words and phrases such as 'I was wondering', 'just,' 'is there any way that,' and 'I was hoping' as well as other expressions and modals highlighted in previous studies. But, they should also be on the lookout for students' creative use of expressions such as 'could you happen to' that students intend as politeness markers, or more specifically mitigators, meant to soften their request and minimize the imposition. Not recognizing them could lead to false conclusions that students do not mean to be polite.

Teachers should not expect highly elaborate expressions of gratitude or apology in request e-mails though they will find that these types of expressions are relatively common and often are used more than once in the same e-mail. Also, whatever a teacher's own personal experience and training in the use of 'please' to accompany requests, it is clear in this analysis that students used this word relatively infrequently in e-mail requests, though they expressed politeness in a variety of other ways.

Finally, teachers should be slow to judge an e-mail as impolite merely on the basis of a lack of typical politeness markers. Rather, they should take into account a student's particular situation and emotional state, as well as the student's use of other polite or at least friendly language (e.g., greetings, salutations, well-wishes, etc.) when evaluating, reacting, and, ultimately, responding to a message. Furthermore, it is important to remember that some students are, unfortunately, accustomed to teachers not responding to e-mail in a timely manner, or at all, while others respond, but not in a helpful manner. This awareness might be reflected in the 'outs' students provide their teachers along with their requests (e.g., 'if you are unable to, I understand'; 'if not, no problem'; 'if this isn't possible, I'll figure out something else'; and 'if I don't hear from you, I'll see you in class'.) Such experiences might lead students to compose messages never truly expecting to receive a response. This could be particularly true in larger, lecture-based classes where it is impossible for a teacher to get to know 50, 100, or even hundreds of students. Nevertheless, in more intimate contexts, teachers should take into account what they know about their students, good and bad, when evaluating the politeness of a particular message. And, when an e-mail request truly is impolite, whether to the teacher who receives it or potentially to others in the future who might receive a similarly-written message, a teacher almost always has the option of using the opportunity to tactfully enlighten the student and sensitize him or her to the particular characteristics that caused the particular message to come off as rude and suggest more polite strategies.

The question of politeness is often quite subjective. What one teacher evaluates as impolite, another might find to be acceptable for many reasons. More and extensive research should be conducted to determine if there are particular strategies that a majority of teachers find to be effective in conveying politeness and other e-mail request features that are considered impolite across the board. Ideally, these investigations will be carried out with real teachers who evaluate real messages, perhaps even from their own students, so that issues of familiarity can be better taken into account in the analysis. And, finally, in line with Lee & Park (2011), much more is to be known about cross-cultural differences in request-making through e-mail.

CHAPTER SIX

Repair Work: Apologies

'I wanted to apologize again for this afternoon. I had consumed an entire bottle of water before the exam and had been trying to hold it in but couldn't handle it anymore. I tried to exit as discretely as possible, but I will make sure in the future that I make eye contact or ask permission. I feel so horrible about it because I had not been thinking at all, I was just listening to my body. In all of the other exams I've taken this year the professors have just told us we could use the bathroom as needed so I didn't think twice about it. Thank you for bringing it to my attention that I need to check/think twice because I had never thought that it could be mistaken for academic dishonesty. I am now tens times more aware of the situation and will avoid it happening again at all costs. Once again I'm really truly sorry and thank you for bringing the issue to my attention. Have a great summer!'

A student's image or face (Brown & Levinson, 1987) can be threatened by social 'transgressions' of various kinds, but, in many cases, these situations can be successfully repaired by an apology. Meier (1997) envisioned 'repair work' (RW), including both apologies and excuses, as a way to 'save the speaker's image when the speaker behaved in some way below the standard expectation relative to a particular reference group' (197).

Interactions in educational institutions are governed by rules and expectations ranging from the enforcement of attendance and academic honesty policies to expectations that students participate in class and behave politely as well as professionally. Students are usually aware that class absences and inappropriate exam conduct carry particular consequences such as grade reductions or more serious penalties. Rarely are infractions in those areas as communicatively complex as other offenses more directly related to student-teacher interaction. However, some problematic situations do prompt students to apologize for a particular behavior that might have damaged their image or standing with the teacher.

An analysis of the current data revealed 267 messages, including both apologies and excuses, through which students engaged in RW. Among these were 197 messages that teachers would recognize as traditional 'absence excuses', 53 others in which students tried to repair previous or even future potentially-offensive behaviors, and 17 e-mails that were interpreted and coded as non-absence-related apologies. These 17 apology messages were analyzed apart from the other 250 RW e-mails for the following three reasons: (1) They were not motivated by a student's class absence; (2) They did not relate to a future offense but rather to one that had already occurred; and, (3) Though some also contained a related question or thank you, the primary reason for which students sent these e-mails was to apologize, not to carry out some other speech act (i.e., make a request, express gratitude, etc.).

For instance, some of the other RW messages included students' explicit apology statements along with other apology routines, but, based on the assumption that teachers are likely to interpret students' absence e-mails as excuses, rather than as legitimate apologies regardless of their actual content, the 197 'absence excuses' were excluded from the analysis of apologies. The explicit apologies included in the other 53 RW messages seemed to be secondary; that is, they constituted a component of excuse routines which were the primary and actual motivation behind the e-mails. They, too, were excluded from the analysis of apologies. Conversely, in the 17 messages on which this chapter is based, excuses were occasionally included but only as part of the overall apology, not as the main purpose of the message. As will be seen more clearly in the following sections, decisions to code a message as an apology or as an excuse were based on the specific repair work students targeted in their messages (absence-related or not) and the analysis of particular linguistic features of the e-mails themselves (e.g., lexical choices, speech act formulas, etc.).

Five Apology Formulas

Much previous research on apologizing has been based on a long-standing framework identified by Olshtain & Cohen (1983) as part of the apology speech act. Specifically, they maintained that an offender uses one or more of the following five apology formulas when he or she feels 'positively inclined to apologize' (22) as opposed to deny all responsibility for an action:

1. Express an apology
2. Explain or give an account of the situation
3. Acknowledge responsibility
4. Offer a repair
5. Promise forbearance

For instance, to express an apology, an offender might use language such as 'I'm sorry' or 'I apologize'. Also, depending on the actual situation, an offender might try to explain what caused the offense in the first place, and might even provide this explanatory account instead of an explicit expression of apology. The offender might additionally include an acknowledgment of responsibility for the offense with language such as 'It is my fault', 'I wasn't thinking', 'You are right!', or 'I didn't mean to'. To try to repair the situation, he or she might offer to make some kind of restitution (e.g., buy a new vase to replace a broken one, etc.). Olshtain & Cohen (1983) added that this fourth formula 'would be relevant only if physical injury or other damage has resulted' (23). Finally, an offender might promise forbearance in the future, especially if the offense could have been avoided: 'It won't happen again'. Though only one of these five formulas need be explicitly included in an apology, Olshtain & Cohen (1983) noted that their combined use creates a higher intensity of apology. Consider, for example, the force of this hypothetical e-mail apology incorporating all the highlighted formulas:

> 'Dear Friend, I'm very sorry (formula #1) for not returning your laptop to you last night and that your girlfriend got mad. Once I got busy, I totally forgot (formula #2) that you needed it to write your history paper. I wasn't thinking (formula #3) about anyone besides myself. I would be happy to tell your girl-friend (formula #4) that it was my fault that you weren't online and to explain (formula #4) what happened. If you are ever willing to lend it to me again, I promise to be more careful (formula #5).'

The combination of more than one routine strengthens an apology, even one made by e-mail.

Although established in the early stages of speech act research, Olshtain & Cohen's (1983) formulas remain a helpful and frequently-used framework for the analysis of apologies. This framework, or a slightly-modified version, has been used to investigate the characteristics of actual apologies or to compare apologies made by native and non-native speakers of different or the same languages (Allami & Naeimi, 2011; Ancarno, 2005; Blum-Kulka, House, & Kasper, 1989; Chang & Haugh, 2011; Hong, 2008; Jebahi, 2011; Kasanga & Lwanga-Lumu, 2007; Kasper & Blum-Kulka, 1993; Lee & Park, 2011; Meier, 1997; Mulamba, 2009; Wagner & Roebuck, 2010). Other investigations have focused on students' acquisition of L2 apology routines and RW (Chang, 2010; Cohen & Shively 2007; Dalmau & Gotor, 2007; Shively & Cohen, 2008). Recently, however, very few studies have specifically explored L1 RW, especially in the context of e-mail discourse (see Ancarno, 2005 and Hong, 2008 for two exceptions).

The linguistic moves to offer to repair a situation and to assure the offended party that the speaker's behavior will improve in the future were also highlighted by Meier (1997). She claimed that RW in general 'repairs the damaged image by reaffirming shared values, thereby assuring the hearer that the speaker is a bona fide member of the group, who can be counted on to act appropriately in the future' (198). Thus, even if physical injury or damage was not caused, an offender might still try to fix a situation by articulating what the interlocutors share in order to regain his or her good standing in the eyes of the one offended. Applied to the academic context, this notion of repair suggests that, as part of an apology, a student might send a late assignment by e-mail, promise not to miss additional classes, or pledge to check e-mail more regularly in the future.

Kasper & Dahl (1991) are two of many researchers who recognized authentic discourse as the best data collection context for research on speech acts. Though Demeter (2007) and others have pointed out possible disadvantages of naturalistic data (most seriously those of variable control and issues of sample size), the numerous benefits of real-life data are difficult to overlook (Ewald, 2012). Thus, in the present investigation, it is important to note that students were never required to apologize to their teacher for any of the situations that prompted their e-mails. All of their apologies were offered voluntarily; that is, they were not collected as a result of discourse completion tasks (DCTs), interviews, or as other types of elicited data (as were the apologies analyzed in Olshtain & Cohen (1983) and Meier (1997), among many others). Though relatively few in number (17), they represent unsolicited apologies offered by real students operating within a naturalistic setting and, as such, comprise a valuable, albeit small, data set. In the following sections, these e-mail apologies will first be analyzed in light of Olshtain and Cohen's (1983) five formulas and then according to Meier's (1997) three supercategories, to be presented later.

1. Expressions of Apology

Students approached the act of apology differently in these 17 e-mails.

For example, one e-mail did not contain an explicit statement at all but six e-mails included two or more apologetic expressions. Specific phrases students used to apologize are presented in Table 6.1.

Table 6.1: Students' Expressions of Apology

Expression of Apology	Frequency of Occurrence
Sorry, I'm (so, really, truly) sorry	15
I (wanted to, sincerely) apologize	6
I (do) feel (really/so) bad/horrible	3
Pardon	1
None of the Above	1

In addition, students used intensifiers (such as 'really', 'truly', 'sincerely', 'so' and 'do') eight times to accompany their 26 expressions of apology. Overall, specific statements of regret (e.g., varieties of 'I'm sorry' and 'I feel bad') were more common than other expressions of apology in this English data, a result that confirms this same finding in both Olshtain & Cohen (1983) and Ancarno (2005).

2. Explanation or Account of the Situation

In the majority of these e-mails (13/17), students offered reasons for their respective offenses, and as predicted by Olshtain & Cohen (1983), their explanations were highly context-dependent. For example, one student explained he had not responded to an e-mail because he had just returned from a trip out of town. The student who sent the e-mail introducing this chapter explained that she had left the classroom during the exam because she physically could not wait any longer to go to the bathroom. Another student accounted for not waiting to talk to the teacher after class (as the teacher had previously requested) because a friend was waiting to take her to pick up her car that had just been repaired after an accident. Finally, one student did not actually explain why he had to reschedule a missed exam but apologized for the situation and offered to provide a more detailed account: 'Long story I can discuss this with you if you would like in person. Let me know.'

Olshtain & Cohen (1983) noted that this formula (i.e., explanation/ account) might be used in place of an explicit expression of apology. This was indeed the case for one student who never actually apologized for her action (having asked a native speaker of Spanish to proofread her composition before she handed it in, an action prohibited in the course syllabus), but wrote an e-mail that was clearly intended to repair the infraction and her image. In sum, many of these students offered explanations of the circumstances surrounding their offenses, some accompanied by an apology.

3. Acknowledgment of Responsibility

Olshtain & Cohen (1983) outlined four ways an offender might acknowledge responsibility for an offense: accepting the blame ('I know I shouldn't have'), expressing self-deficiency ('I was confused'), recognizing the other person as deserving an apology ('you have every right to be upset') and expressing a lack of intent ('I didn't mean for it to turn out this way'). In 11 of these 17 e-mails, students directly accepted blame for their actions by using phrases that acknowledged the offensiveness, or at least potential offensiveness, of their conduct, in that they had arrived late or not at all, behaved inappropriately, or submitted unacceptable work. This is not to suggest that the other six students did not acknowledge responsibility for their actions; obviously, the fact that they voluntarily e-mailed their teacher represents some recognition of personal responsibility on their part, at least for the situation if not for their actual behaviors. The other six apologies were worded in such a way as either to imply responsibility or to express ownership of the situation. For example, one student had not seen an e-mail in time to respond accordingly. To repair the resulting misunderstanding, she apologized by e-mail with this explanation, 'sorry I didn't get the e-mail before class, however I had [a class right before our class] today also.' Her message did not explicitly acknowledge responsibility for not having read the previous e-mail but her account of the situation implied that she had not read it and also explained why.

4. An Offer of Repair

It is noteworthy that in over half (59%) of these messages, though none of them involved 'physical injury or other damage' (Olshtain & Cohen, 1983), students still made specific offers to repair the problematic situations they had created and tried to 'make up for' their particular offenses (see Table 6.2). For example, they offered to meet with the teacher at a mutually convenient time or to discuss their situations further. One promised to put more time into other assignments and another guaranteed she would e-mail a missing document to the teacher that same night. One even offered to do anything that the teacher suggested might 'make up for it'. Their repair offers are significant for at least two reasons: first, they had nothing to do with having damaged the 'offended' party (i.e., the teacher) but rather to having possibly damaged their own image as students, a scenario not mentioned by Olshtain & Cohen (1983); and second, for the most part, their offers of repair were specifically related to the actual circumstances that they themselves perceived to require repair, a practice expected when managing face-threatening situations (Brown & Levinson, 1987).

Table 6.2: Students' Offers of Repairs

	Apologies Including a Specific Offer of Repair	Apologies Without an Offer of Repair
Totals	10	7
	17	

Olshtain & Cohen (1983) emphasized that this formula, along with the next (a promise of forbearance) can occur 'only if the specific discourse situation calls for such formulas' (23). This was indeed the case in these data. That is, the offenses committed by the students who did not offer a repair were of a different nature and could not be 'fixed' in such practical ways. For example, a person is unable to go back in time to read an e-mail sooner, to not send an e-mail to the wrong person, to be physically present for an event or class in the past, or to not leave a classroom during an exam that already took place. Illogical repairs were not offered by these students. In fact, their intentional and reasonable moves to repair the situations affirmed Meier's (1997) claim that RW is 'an interpersonal mediator of image, reinstating the good standing of a group member who has violated a social norm' (198) as well as her claim that repairs often reaffirm shared values between the offender and offended. In all of these apologies, the social norms that had been violated were classroom-related; thus, repairs were offered in such a way as to communicate to the teacher the students' recognition that handing in documents on time and doing one's best work on assignments were important. Their e-mails revealed a desire to ensure a positive image of themselves for their teacher. For two of them, this desire played out in the fifth apology formula, a promise of forbearance.

5. A Promise of Forbearance

As part of their apologies, two students included specific statements that communicated their determination not to repeat the offense in the future. For instance, the introductory message of this chapter (about not leaving a classroom without permission during an exam) contained the sentence 'I am now tens times more aware of the situation and will avoid it happening at all costs'. Another student's offer of repair 'I just wanted to let you know Im going to try and do the best that I can and now ... I will be able to put some more time into the class' indirectly sets up the expectation that his performance on assignments would improve in the future. Though relatively uncommon, these remarks suggest that students recognized that repeating the offenses was unacceptable and would, in turn, negatively affect their image.

As claimed by both Olshtain & Cohen (1983) and Meier (1997), any type of repair work is highly situation-dependent. These students' choices of apology formulas reflected their specific circumstances as well as their sense of responsibility for their respective offenses.

Three 'Supercategories'

Meier (1997) outlined what she called three 'supercategories' adapted from Snyder, Higgins and Stucky's (1983) research on excuses. In their book, 'Excuses: Masquerades in Search of Grace', they attempted to develop a descriptive model of excuses based on both social and psychological considerations. Meier (1997) then applied these categories to a linguistic analysis to explore the role that cultural attitudes and contextual factors play in excuse-making. The three categories are the following: (1) reinstate the positive image of the offender, (2) make the speaker's position understandable to the hearer, and (3) help the speaker and hearer meet halfway. Each will be described in detail.

As previously mentioned, Meier's (1997) first main point was that an offender uses repair language to bring about convergence between him/herself and the offended party, thus reinstating the positive image of the offender. Specifically, a speaker might say something like 'I know that this is totally unpleasant for you' in order to show that s/he understands the position of the hearer and appreciates the hearer's feelings. This supercategory is quite similar to one expression of the third formula of Olshtain & Cohen (1983) in which an offender acknowledges blame by recognizing explicitly that the other person deserves an apology, a technique not used in the present apology data. Given students' recognition that their behaviors ultimately affect themselves and not their teacher, the absence of this particular type of blame acknowledgment is not surprising. That is, as a student apologizes for not submitting an assignment on time, it would be somewhat odd to include statements like 'I know this is discouraging to you' or 'Even if you will accept my paper, I know this timing complicates your grading'. While both may be true, the social distance in the hierarchical student-teacher relationship likely complicates or reduces the options available to students when apologizing.

Meier's (1997) second supercategory involves statements such as 'but you know anyway how that always is' that are meant to make the speaker's position understandable to the hearer. This supercategory seems most closely related to Olshtain and Cohen's (1983) second formula, that of providing the offended party with an explanation or an account of a situation; in other words, the explanation is intended to help the hearer comprehend the speaker's situation well enough to understand the offense in the context in which it was committed. In the present data, the students' explanations were detailed enough to draw on their teacher's shared knowledge of what real life is like. For instance, relatives do have car accidents and need help, repaired vehicles should be picked up from the garage, and, eventually, one must go to the bathroom! The acceptability of students' accounts depends on their teacher's 'knowing how that is' and agreeing, at least to some extent, with their actions.

Finally, Meier's (1997) third supercategory accounts for statements such as 'I hope this won't affect our friendship' or 'forgive me' that are intended to help the speaker and the hearer meet halfway with the focus of the interaction being on 'absolution, that is, an attempt to wipe the slate clean' (198). In the present study, this third supercategory was most visible in two areas: (1) students' promises of forbearance (Olshtain & Cohen's (1983) fifth formula), and (2) their offers of repair (Olshtain & Cohen's (1983) fourth formula) in which they made specific suggestions to counter or mitigate the damage caused by their offense (i.e., e-mail a document, meet in person later, etc.). As was documented previously, in the first area, students' promises of forbearance directly attempted to assure the teacher that they could be trusted in the future, and, in the second, their offers of repair were directly aimed at wiping the slate clean in related, practical ways.

The Compatibility of the Five Formulas with the Three Supercategories

Meier's (1997) supercategories describing the desired convergence between speaker and hearer took into account the possibility that a speaker's RW might include actual statements of justification or excuse. Based on the work of Scott & Lyman (1968), she distinguished justifications, *acceptances* of responsibility, from excuses, *denials* of responsibility. Unlike justifications, excuses 'attempt to show that an actor's real intent or will was interfered with by a force for which she or he could not be held responsible' (202). Potentially in contrast, Olshtain & Cohen's (1983) framework, as mentioned at the beginning of this chapter, describes moments when 'the offender perceived the need to apologize' (22) and felt 'positively inclined to apologize' (22), rather than deny all responsibility for an action. Initially, these two frameworks for analyzing apologies seem to be incompatible since an excuse that denies responsibility (Meier) seems logically unlikely to co-occur with an apology motivated by the need to apologize (Olshtain & Cohen). However, more careful consideration shows them to be quite complementary.

Olshtain & Cohen (1983) claimed that an offender might reject the need to apologize by using language such as 'there was no need for you to get insulted', or by either refusing to accept the blame outright, 'It wasn't my fault', or by casting blame on the offended party, 'It's your own fault' (23). An excuse may or may not logically accompany any one of these three scenarios. Consider, for example, the following situations in which the speakers reject the need to apologize and provide related excuses: 'There was no need for you to get insulted. You know I was tired when I said your outfit looked funny and that when I'm tired I say things I don't mean.'; 'It wasn't my fault that your car was damaged. The other guy ran into me while I was just sitting at the light.'; and, 'It's your own fault that your cell phone doesn't work. You left it by the sink last night and in the dark, how was I supposed to know it was there?!'. Thus, excuses can be completely independent of apologies.

Conversely, excuses can accompany apologies. Olshtain & Cohen (1983) did not claim that a speaker who follows the apology formulas automatically assumes all responsibility for the offense, but that he or she perceives the need to apologize, whether or not that need is legitimate or whether or not the speaker sees him/herself as fully to blame. What they termed 'indirect expressions of responsibility' (23) could entail speakers' attempts to repair their image with the hearer by using language that is sufficiently sincere to 'set things right' but vague enough to fail (deliberately) to accept total responsibility for the offense. Thus, when an offender explains or offers an account of a situation (i.e., provides an excuse), the speaker might actually be attempting to help the hearer understand his/her situation better (Meier's (1997) second supercategory), by inviting the hearer to recognize that there were forces 'for which she or he could not be held responsible' (Meier, 1997: 202). In this way, excuses, as defined by Meier (1997) as 'denials of responsibility', do fit within and affirm the usefulness and validity of Olshtain & Cohen's (1983) framework.

In support of this argument, Meier (1997) found that her participants frequently admitted offense while simultaneously providing justifications for their actions; moreover, they also made excuses and offered justifications for their actions at the same time despite the somewhat contradictory nature of these repair work strategies (RWSs). She claimed, 'These results thus support a functional rather than propositional view of RWSs in the sense that although the claims may be contradictory, their function in repairing a damaged identity is the same. It is this commonality of function that allows for their cooccurrence' (201).

Though the students in the present study apologized for their respective offenses, their language included excuses (denials of responsibility), justifications (acceptances of responsibility), and both. For example, the student who wrote 'sorry I didn't get the e-mail before class, however I had [a class right before our class] today also' apologized for her failure to read a previous e-mail; at the same time, she also denied responsibility for her offense due to a situation for which she could not be held responsible (i.e., attending another class). Similarly, another student apologized for having missed an appointment but explained 'I'm actually at home right now, I got a call this morning that my aunt had an accident and my mom needed me to come stay with my cousins while she took her to the hospital ... bad timing right?'. Her addition of the phrase 'bad timing, right?' suggests her awareness that, as for other students and their excuses, the legitimacy and acceptability of an excuse depends, at least in part, on her teacher's evaluation of the situation and its severity, an issue that will be revisited in Chapter 7.

Other students' apologies included both an excuse and a justification as part of the same message. For example, the student who had asked the native speaker of Spanish to proofread her composition before she handed it in denied responsibility for her decision with the excuse 'I did not know that it was not okay for my paper to be proof read by someone outside of the class'. She acknowledged understanding the situation, 'I understand why I need to write the paper over again', but tried to justify her poor decision by saying 'I actually thought that it would be beneficial for me to have it proof read by someone who is in a higher level Spanish class than myself'. All this RW was aimed to repair the negative image of herself she feared she had created for her teacher, and her message closed with the frank acknowledgment, 'I hope that this misunderstanding does not change your opinion of me as a student'. As posited by Meier (1997), though the claims behind an excuse and a justification may be contradictory, together they function to repair a damaged identity, the purpose of the apology in its entirety.

The apology/excuse/justification combination is also evident in the message introducing this chapter. That student first explicitly apologized for having left the classroom during an exam without permission ('I wanted to apologize again for this afternoon'), denied responsibility for the action ('[I] couldn't handle it anymore') and then justified her decision to leave by stating 'In all of the other exams I've taken this year the professors have just told us we could use the bathroom as needed so I didn't think twice about it.' By appealing to her experiences with other teachers she attempted to portray the offense as less serious. All together, her apology, excuse and justification functioned as RW.

Within RW, the lines separating these speech acts fall very closely together. At first glance, it would seem easy to distinguish an apology (involving an acknowledgment of blame) from an excuse (involving a denial of responsibility); but, as noted in Olshtain (1989) and Ruzaitė & Čubajevaitė (2007), the situation is often not so transparent. Some offenders incorporate '*but*-explanations' in their apologies, perhaps to minimize the seriousness of the offense or, as seen in Olshtain

& Cohen (1983), Meier (1997), and the present data, to help the listener better understand the situation. Furthermore, the distinction between excuses (denials of responsibility) and justifications (acceptances of responsibility) is often not clear-cut either. For example, when students compose e-mail absence 'excuses', they sometimes claim that their absence is due to a situation beyond their control (e.g., 'I apologize for missing todays class, Thursday, February 5th at 2:30. I was in a meeting with [a university administrator] and it went longer than expected. I know that you allow us to miss a couple classes but I felt that you deserved an explanation.'); at other times, students' absence 'excuses' read more like justifications in the sense that they try to portray their absence as a good thing (e.g., 'My best friend was in a really bad car accident. She was thrown through the windshield of the car and is now in the hospital in a coma and on a respirator. Things aren't looking good right now and I had to be home for moral support with her family and my other friends from home.'). In both of these cases, even though their absences would not be held against them, these students accepted responsibility for having missed class but accounted for their absences by pointing to forces beyond their control (the meeting excuse) and to competing social obligations (the helping family/friends justification). Thus, as claimed by Meier (1997), given their inherent complexities and significant differences, specific situations for which people engage in RW require detailed, context-specific investigations, a recommended area for future research addressed in Chapter 7.

Pedagogical Implications and Future Research

Particularly related to students' e-mail apologies are the following pedagogical implications and corresponding areas for future research. First, teachers should recognize that students feel vulnerable given the unequal power relationship that characterizes educational settings. Having committed an offense, whether legitimately at fault or not, many students recognize the face-threatening potential of such situations and some, voluntarily, seek to mitigate the damage they might have caused by composing e-mail apologies. Teachers should recognize and appreciate that sense of vulnerability and respond accordingly. Specifically, when appropriate, apologizing students would benefit from teacher responses that communicate successful repairs have taken place. For example, teacher e-mails including statements such as 'Thanks for your apology, I appreciate it.', 'We can talk more in person but meeting instead on Friday would be fine.', or 'No problem about not seeing my previous e-mail while you were in class. No harm done.' would likely go a long way toward alleviating students' concerns about having offended or alienated their teachers. Of course, appropriate responses vary according to the specific circum-stances, but teachers, perhaps especially those who express displeasure over stu-dents' lack of decorum and professional interactions, should consider the message communicated to students when sincere apologies are met with silence. Moreover, teachers should be sensitive to the various formulas students use in their e-mail apologies and pay special attention to the presence of intensifiers and multiple for-mulas in one message. Rather than being annoyed by students' sometimes long-winded accounts of their circumstances, teachers should interpret these detailed explanations as students' attempts to help them understand why they committed a particular offense. That does not mean that teachers should expend time and/or energy analyzing the details of an account to determine its validity. Nevertheless, simple statements such as 'I hope your aunt is okay.' or 'I understand why you thought that a native speaker editor might be helpful but you will benefit more from rewriting the paper on your own.' affirm students' attempts at RW.

Almost 60% of these students' apologies included their attempts to repair sit-uations by proposing specific ideas. If a teacher does not approve students' own suggestions, s/he might still recognize the good intentions mostly likely behind them, and, when appropriate, suggest a more suitable alternative. Even if the pro-posed 'repair' does not completely make up for the offense, allowing students to mitigate the damage as much as possible allows them to regain face with their teacher, and this, in turn, could lead toward a more productive relationship in future interactions.

Finally, students do have non-academic obligations to their family, friends, roommates, and jobs, as well as various other commitments and interests. That is not to say that they become less responsible for their coursework if someone they know is in crisis or if they do not complete an assignment because of other respon-sibilities. However, educators themselves frequently juggle multiple tasks and roles and should be sensitive to students who are learning to do the same as they take on adult roles and responsibilities. Supporting them as they develop while holding them accountable for course obligations is a challenging task that requires con-stant readjustments with individual students and situations. When students use apologetic language that both justifies and excuses their actions, teachers might note the competing tensions students are experiencing and use those moments as opportunities to help them learn to balance all these demands. Since most sin-cere apologies are, inherently, acknowledgments of responsibility for one's actions, teachers should maintain an appropriate level of sensitivity to students' needs and situations, especially when they apologize for an offense.

To improve pedagogical interactions, future research on e-mail apologies could explore any number of those issues. Particularly enlightening would be investigations that are able to help educators better understand their own reactions and responses to students' e-mailed apologies as well as studies that analyze teachers' individualized interpretations of students' apology strategies. Though faculty, particularly at the university level, may feel that the approach advocated here is more appropriate to K-12 education, more and more students enter post-secondary education without the communicative skills and know-how required to manage apologies in these kinds of formal, hierarchical settings. Such matters raise larger issues about society's goals for its educational system and teachers' own beliefs about their responsibilities and roles at various levels of instruction. Obviously, teachers must make their own decisions about how to respond to students' apologies. Considering the pragmatic characteristics of students' e-mail apologies provides more information for arriving at conclusions with which one feels comfortable.

CHAPTER SEVEN

Repair Work: Excuses

'I am about to come to campus for the first time this week. I'm starting to feel a little better. I had to go to the hospital last night because i couldn't take it anymore. The x-rays showed that I have another kidney stone making its way to my bladder. I thought it was food poisoning or bacteria from some wings I ate on Sunday during the game. I will drop my work off at your office. Will you be in your office tomorrow? If so, I will stop by when you're there. Otherwise, will you be there on Thursday at or before 11:30? I just want to go over what I missed. Thank you.'

'That's an excuse, not a reason!' How many times have children or students received this or a similar response to an account they have provided for their actions? If they had studied pragmatics, they would be better equipped to explain that though an excuse denies their perceived responsibility for an action (Meier, 1997), it does indeed constitute a reason for their potentially offensive behavior. Thus, the parent's or teacher's response should technically be 'That's an excuse and a reason but you are still responsible for your actions!'

However, the notion of responsibility itself is actually quite complex. If a student chooses to miss class in order not to offend a university administrator with whom he is meeting, is the student actually responsible for his absence? Or, if another student fails to attend class because she has chosen to be with family and friends who are suffering, does her commitment to them outweigh her responsibility to be in class? Answers to these questions are often provided by teachers through gradebook notations indicating an 'excused' or 'permitted' absence or, in contrast, a reduction in a student's grade. As suggested by Hong (2008), the legitimacy and acceptability of an excuse depends, at least in part, on the teacher's evaluation of the student's situation.

Some Excuse Origins

One common origin for excuses is blame. For example, after breaking up a fight a police officer might ask the participants what happened. As soon as blame begins to be assigned, both parties attempt to defend themselves, perhaps by excusing the punches each one has thrown on the basis of what the other did first (a denial of responsibility related to self-defense) or by justifying the punches on the grounds of protecting a third party who was the real target of one of the participants (an acceptance of responsibility that attempts to portray one's behavior 'as less offensive or as positive' (Meier, 1997: 203)).

Excuses can also come about when someone *feels* blamed even though no blame has been explicitly cast. For instance, having failed to wash last night's dirty dishes stacked in the sink, one roommate might notice the knowing look he receives from the other and respond with the following excuse: 'Look, my friends didn't leave until really late and I was exhausted. I'll take care of them now.' Or, even without the roommate's 'look,' based on their shared expectations, he might still provide the same excuse simply when his roommate enters the kitchen. In this case, his excuse is meant proactively to prevent an accusation or a complaint rather than to respond after blame had already been assigned.

In addition to those brought on by past actions, excuses also surface as responses to requests or invitations for present and future events. For example, in their comparison of English and Persian speech acts, Allami & Naeimi (2011) used discourse completion tasks (DCTs) to elicit L1 and L2 refusal data. Specific contexts included the following: turning down a boss's invitation to a party, declining a cleaning lady's offer to replace a broken vase, and rejecting a friend's suggestion to try a new diet. Among other strategies, L1 English subjects frequently used excuses to communicate their refusals. For example, one responded to the boss's party invitation with the following: 'I had a prior commitment and since you just told me now, and my shift usually ends at seven, I probably can't stay late this evening' (392). In general, Allami & Naeimi (2011) found excuses to constitute specific, concrete, and to-the-point reasons for the participants' refusals.

Terminology: Reasons, Excuses, Justifications or Appeals

Envisioning excuses as reasons underpins the general understanding and function of an 'absence excuse' in academic contexts. An absence excuse attempts to explain why a student was, is or will be absent from class. Though some researchers (Meier, 1997) emphasize that an excuse technically represents a denial of responsibility, most students would probably prefer that teachers interpret their absence excuses, and all of their excuses for that matter, as legitimate and acceptable explanations rather than as rejections of accountability. Certainly, if the tone of an e-mail excuse communicates to a professor that a student feels little or no responsibility for his or her own learning, the teacher's interpretation of that excuse will most likely be negative. On the other hand, if a student successfully communicates genuine competence, dependability, and concern for a class while simultaneously explaining an absence or the submission of a late assignment, the excuse will more likely be interpreted by the teacher in positive terms, depending on the situation, professor's expectation and academic policies at play.

As discussed in Chapter 6, an important distinction in repair work (RW) can be drawn between excuses, or denials of responsibility, and justifications, or acceptances of responsibility (Meier, 1997). Meier explained that 'justifications are an attempt to portray offensive behavior as less offensive or as positive' (203). Her characterization of excuses involves an attempt to 'show that an actor's real intent or will was interfered with by a force for which she or he could not be held responsible (Scott & Lyman, 1968). Therefore, the more one can plead lack of responsibility, the less one can be held to blame' (Meier, 1997: 202).

Scott & Lyman (1968) provided a four-way distinction to account for the formulation of excuses: (1) appeal to accidents; (2) appeal to defeasibility; (3) appeal to biological drives; and (4) scapegoating. While perhaps useful in sociological studies, this framework does not provide a complete account of students' e-mail excuses. It appears that the e-mail context itself provides new avenues for appeal, thereby signaling a significant change within societal norms due to the influence of technology. The present investigation responds to Meier's (1997) conclusion that specific *situations* for which people engage in RW require their own detailed investigations; it should be added that specific *mediums* through which people engage in RW also require an individualized analysis. Thus, this chapter first explores RW related to class absences communicated through the medium of e-mail.

E-mail Apology Strategies Viewed Cross-Culturally

Before analyzing the present data, it is important to review another existing study of student RW e-mails related to class absences. Hong (2008) investigated the apology strategies used by English L1 and L2 students in e-mail correspondence regarding their absences. Her findings were based on naturalistic data, specifically e-mails written by 59 university students enrolled in two separate classes: a technology class (TC) and a Chinese language class (CC). The 33 TC students were all L1 speakers of English; 16 of the 26 CC students were L1 speakers of English though the other 10 were L1 speakers of various Asian languages and L2 speakers of English. Hong (2008) reported that 85% of the CC students 'were from Asia or ha[d] Chinese heritage' (152). According to their respective course syllabi, both the TC and the CC students were required to attend all class sessions and to report any absences in writing in order to be excused by their teachers. Hong (2008) found what she believed to be a higher degree of politeness in the e-mails of the

CC students who had been exposed, at varying degrees, to Chinese cultural norms according to which class absences are considered disrespectful to the teacher. Thus, for the CC students, the severity of the offense of missing class was assumed to be greater which, in turn, resulted in their use of different apology strategies.

Among other apology-related findings, Hong (2008) discovered that most students explained their absences by appealing to one of the following three categories: personal, medical or professional. Though, she did not distinguish 'excuses' from 'justifications,' but viewed them all as explanations, her three-way categorization of the students' accounts is useful. In the TC and CC e-mails, 91% and 100% respectively, provided explanations for their absences. The differences found in their explanation categories are noteworthy (see Table 7.1).

Table 7.1: Explanation Categories of Class Absences (Hong, 2008)

Explanation Category	TC	CC
Personal	37%	15%
Professional	33%	12%
Medical	30%	73%

Specifically, Hong (2008) found that more of the CC students' e-mails (73%) cited a medical reason as the cause of their absences; on the other hand, more of the TC students (37%) pointed to personal reasons. Overall, she concluded that both groups of students recognized the need to explain their absences.

However, several limitations were not addressed in this study. First, both groups of students were told to report their absences; that is, though the students chose to send their absence e-mails and decided what to write, the e-mails themselves were not entirely voluntary in nature. Moreover, the syllabus instructions in each of these classes were not identical. In the TC class, students were told that their e-mails must provide 'the instructor advance notification of the absence and its justification' (161). They were also allowed an expressed maximum of three excused absences and received a 3% grade deduction for each unexcused absence. In the CC class, no mention of (un)excused absences was included in the syllabus and students were simply informed, 'Absences should be promptly reported in writing to the instructor' and that 'Late arrivals should be justified to the instructor after class' (162). Given these important differences, the expectations held by these two groups of students were likely very different and, in turn, may have affected their absence e-mails in various ways. Finally, given that the two teachers were different people and that most of these students (specifically, 49/59) were L1 speakers of English, it is likely, and even taken for granted by the author who emphasized that students in the CC group studied 'under the influence of Asian culture' (153), that the students were also affected by their respective teacher's oral instructions and expectations regarding both absences and communicative norms. Nevertheless, Hong's (2008) documentation of the reasons for students' absences provides a useful point of comparison with the present data.

The Present Study: Repair Work E-mails

Excluding the 17 apologies analyzed in Chapter 6, the present data contain a total of 250 RW e-mails: 197 absence e-mails and 53 other RW messages in which students tried to account for previous (7) or future (46) behaviors. Though many of these messages contained specific expressions of apology and incorporated other apology formulas, they were analyzed apart from the 17 apologies on the basis of the following three criteria: (1) they were motivated by a student's class absence (as in the case of the 197 absence e-mails); or, (2) they related to a previous offense but did not constitute an apology (7 e-mails); or, (3) they related to a future offense but did not constitute an apology (46 e-mails). Thus, as will be seen below, though there is clear overlap between apology and excuse e-mails, it was useful to analyze them separately.

Attendance Policy

> *'I might be going home early for the services of my friend who passed away this week. I believe I have one absence, but I wanted to make sure that was accurate. Thank you so much.'*

Depending on their actual class meeting schedule (two or three class sessions per week), students in the present study had been informed that either two or three absences were automatically excused; several of their messages documented their awareness of those terms. The teacher's attendance policy was strict in that students were expected to be in class and were assigned a class participation grade based minimally on their attendance record but primarily on their engagement during small and whole group activities and overall level of homework preparation. Daily attendance was taken through the distribution of a sign-in sheet. Students were directed to spend their absences as an employee might use sick or personal days and were encouraged to use them wisely so that they would be available when a student was ill, needed to attend a funeral, or wanted to miss class for any reason. The teacher made it clear that she would not judge between 'excused' or 'unexcused' absences but that students were permitted to miss class a designated number of times for any reason without providing any sort of documentation or official justification. Following is the attendance statement from one of the course syllabi during the period of data collection (others were similar, if not identical):

> 'Your participation and your learning depend on your attendance. Therefore, a maximum of 2 absences are permitted. Additional absences will result in a lower grade or in failing the course.'

Thus, though it is possible that students had not read or had forgotten the specifics of this attendance policy by the time they missed a class, they were not required to report an absence or to offer any justification. As a result, unlike the accounts studied in Hong (2008), these 197 absence e-mails collected were voluntary in nature. Perhaps motivated primarily by a desire to create or maintain a positive image, students composed and sent these messages of their own accord. In addition to the student whose message asking about the number of his previous absences introduced this section, other students' e-mails contained language indicating that they were aware of their right to use their absences 'as needed'. For instance, these statements illustrate the way with which some students confidently expressed their intention to be absent: 'On Thursday, April 8, I will not be in class. I am leaving in the morning for Florida for the long weekend.'; 'I just wanted to let you know that I will not be able to attend class on Thursday, October 13 because I am going away.'; and, 'I will not be able to attend class on Thursday March 31 because I will be in New York for the basketball game.'

Timing of Absence E-mails

> *'I am sorry I won't be able to make it to class today, I have a family emergency and im going home. Sorry for the late notice, I just found out myself.'*

Though students were not required to document their absences, the example above is representative of the 102 e-mails that provided the teacher with advance notice of a definite absence or a possibly-upcoming absence (i.e., 'I might not make it'; 'if I'm not there', etc.). In addition, 91 other e-mails addressed an absence that was either currently taking place (i.e., 'Sorry I'm not in class right now') or had recently taken place (e.g., 'I apologize for missing class yesterday').[1] Another timing-related

---

1   In four messages, it was not clear from the wording of the e-mail if the absence had already taken place or was yet to come.

issue had to do with when the actual absence e-mail was sent, an issue some-times also addressed in students' messages. Specifically, in 17 messages, students acknowledged, and most apologized for, the 'late notice' of their absences; these messages included both e-mails sent prior to (10) the absence as well as those sent afterwards (7).

Use of Apology Formulas in Absence E-mails

> *'I apologize for missing class this morning I know I should have been there and I really had all intentions of going. I do not even have good excuse as to why I was absent, I set my alarm for pm and it did not go off and I over slept, and I know this is entirly my falt. Is there any material that I should go over during the break to catch up, and also is their any assignments due for when we return from break. Thank you for your patients and have a safe and happy thanksgiving.'*

As can be seen in the message above, and as was previously mentioned, these 197 e-mails contained many examples of the five apology formulas (Olshtain & Cohen, 1983) outlined in Chapter 6 to communicate absence-related information to the teacher (see Table 7.2 for the number of e-mails that included at least one occurrence of the indicated formulas). In fact, as the percentages below indicate, individual messages often contained more than one formula.

Table 7.2: Students' Use of Apology Formulas in Absence E-mails

Apology Formula	# of E-mails
Expression of Apology	100 (51%)
Explanation or Account of Situation	190 (96%)
Acknowledgment of Responsibility	17 (9%)
Offer of Repair	150 (76%)
Promise of Forbearance	41 (21%)

In 100 messages (51%) students included at least one expression of apology (e.g., 'I'm sorry', 'I apologize', etc.) in the e-mail. Seventy e-mails contained one expression of apology, 26 included two expressions and four included three expres-sions which provided a grand total of 134 expressions of apology in these data. Only seven absence e-mails lacked an explanation or account of the absence; 190 (96%) messages included some sort of reason, be it excuse or justification (more on that below), for the student's absence. In 17 messages, even after having provided an explanation or account, students acknowledged responsibility for the absence in some way (e.g., 'It was my fault'; 'It was a bone head mistake'; 'I am an idiot'; or, 'I did not intend to miss class.'). A large percentage (76%) of these students offered to repair the offense in some way. Given the nature of these messages, logical repairs included offers or promises to provide the teacher with official (though unrequired) documentation of the absence (e.g., doctor's note, etc.), submit an assignment by e-mail or in person, contact a classmate for lecture notes, actually attend class if circumstances allowed (e.g., 'if I'm not sick tomorrow', 'if the roads aren't too bad', etc.), and to complete whatever assignments were due for the following class. Finally, 41 messages (21%) included students' promises of forbearance. Since their offense was missing class, the most common were students' assurances that they would be in class the following session (e.g., 'But I will see you on Thursday') and did not plan to be absent often (e.g., 'This is the last time I will be missing your class for the rest of the semester, I promise'); in other words, though their e-mails acknowledged their absences, many felt compelled to guarantee that they would be in class again as soon as possible.

Though teachers may be prone to interpret students' absence e-mails as 'excuses', these students' actual messages shared many features of apologies. In fact, there was only one message in which a student did not include at least one of the apology formulas mentioned above and that message was sent as a reminder about an upcoming absence that the student and teacher had already discussed in person. Thus, apology routines were used consistently in these absence e-mails. Moreover, even when excluding the most common apology formula (providing an explanation or account) from the analysis, 109 of these messages (55%) included one or more of the other four routines more than once, and many used a few in combination.

That said, just half (51% of these students' messages included explicit expressions of apologies. As pointed out by Olshtain & Cohen (1983), an apology might incorporate any one of these routines or a combination of them to intensify the sentiment. Especially since two of the other formulas were used at such high frequencies (96% and 76%, respectively), it is noteworthy that almost half of these messages did *not* include any specific expression of apology as well as indicates that many of the apology routines were, indeed, used in combination. At least in a course context where absence documentation is not required, it may be that an absence e-mail does not actually constitute an attempt 'to apologize', at least as viewed in a traditional way, but rather represents another form of RW (e.g., 'to account for' or 'to report') that consists of some combination of expression(s) of apology, explanation or account of the situation, and offer(s) of repair. In these 'absence *accounts*' the most common combination of formulas was that of expression of apology + explanation or account of the situation + offer of repair (71 occurrences); the second most common combination was that of explanation or account of the situation + offer of repair (64 occurrences) and the distant third was expression of apology + explanation or account of the situation (24 occurrences). Thus, as suggested by Meier (1997), this analysis demonstrated that distinct RW situations should be studied separately to determine the particular strategies speakers use to engage in repair.

Absence Accounts: Excuses or Justifications?

> 'My little brother overdosed on anti-depressants on Wednesday. I have been with my family since this incident. It looks as though I will be missing class on Thursday. I am truly sorry, but as of right now my priorities are with my family.'

An absence 'account' can also be understood as a student's attempt to protect or repair his or her image with the teacher. In fact, some of these students' accounts even included statements directly pertaining to this particular concern such as 'I really do not want you to get the wrong idea about me or my work ethic'. Meier's (1997) distinction between excuses (denials of responsibility) and justifications (acceptances of responsibility) sheds light on these data.

Before analyzing the present data in view of Meier's (1997) distinction, it should be pointed out that Olshtain & Cohen's third apology formula (acknowledgment of responsibility) does not automatically lead a speaker to justify (i.e., to accept responsibility) in the sense Meier (1997) argued. She defined a justification as 'an attempt to portray offensive behavior as less offensive or as positive' (203); that is, a speaker accepts responsibility for a situation but tries to put a positive spin on it so that it is seen in a more favorable or complimentary light. Olshtain & Cohen's (1983) third formula is meant to account for a speaker's utterances that merely take responsibility for the offense by accepting blame, expressing self-deficiency, recognizing the other person as deserving an apology or expressing a lack of intent, but not those aimed directly at changing the listener's view of the offense explanation provided, recognized to be the primary goal of a justification.

With that important distinction in mind, the analysis of the present data showed that 173 (88%) students' absence e-mails were 'excuses' (denials of responsibility); 17 (9%) were 'justifications' (acceptances of responsibility) and, as mentioned before, seven (3%) did not provide any explanation of the absence and could not therefore be categorized as either excuses or justifications. Despite the seeming contradictions in their claims, a speaker's admission of an offense does not preclude the speaker from trying to remove its offensive potential, nor does the offering of an excuse prevent a speaker from simultaneously accepting responsibility for his or her actions (Meier, 1997). The same phenomena were found in these data. Specifically, though 51% of these e-mails contained at least one expression of apology and all but one of their messages incorporated at least one apology formula, 173 messages also included excuses. That is, though students admitted their offense (i.e., a class absence), many attempted to deny responsibility for it on the basis of a variety of factors that genuinely could and do prevent students from attending class. Moreover, in each of the 17 cases of justification e-mails, students' attempts to portray their absences as less offensive or even as positive were based on circumstantial details they included in the e-mail.

For example, the following student not only pointed to her illness as an unavoidable excuse for her missing class, she also justified her absence in the name of protecting her classmates: 'I apologize for not being in class today and for this late notice. I am feeling sick [an excuse] and I didn't want to infect the rest of the class [a justification].' Another who was ill claimed that not attending class allowed him to 'use all my strength for [an English Honors Society speech tonight] since we have been working on this ceremony for most of the year,' and another was worried that she was 'going to get worse and lose my voice for the play this weekend'. One student attempted to put a positive spin on her absence due to attending a sporting event: '[T]his once in a lifetime opportunity came about. My transportation, hotel and tickets for the games are all paid for, so I hope you understand!'. Like the much more serious drug-overdose context of the student whose message introduced this section, another student explained that she would be absent because she had a doctor's appointment. She justified her need to follow through with the appointment by claiming 'it is very important that I get to it because I will be receiving surgery in June. I hope you understand.'

Students' attempts to help their teacher not only understand but also accept their absence accounts are tied to their desires to be seen as 'good students' who do well in class, stay home when sick, act in plays, participate in honor societies, attend once-in-a-lifetime events, follow through with serious doctor's appointments and help their families in times of crisis. Their resulting justifications were aimed at creating understanding or convergence between the teacher and themselves as they repaired the offenses by casting them in a positive light. By accepting responsibility for their absences while trying to justify their decisions, they sought to restore their image.

Absence Accounts: Categories of Excuses

'Sorry again about today, id say blame the guy who hit me at 40 mph, pushed me into an intersection and almost into cross traffic, and then sped off after yelling at me about it being my fault.'

Like the justification e-mails, the 173 excuse e-mails were also aimed at attracting the understanding of the teacher, but in these cases, students implied (or explicitly stated, as in the e-mail above) that their absences were not their fault but were due to factors beyond their control. In other words, their 'real intent or will [to attend class] was interfered with by a force for which [they] could not be held responsible' (Meier, 1997: 202). That is, they were not responsible for missing class and, consequently, should be blamed less or not at all. For example, in the message above, the student suggested that her teacher blame the driver of the other car who, she said, had incorrectly blamed her!

All of these students' absence accounts suggested, either implicitly or explicitly, that blame for their absences should be assigned to either animate or inanimate 'others'. These 'others' included the mom who says 'I am in no condition to be anywhere but home,' the nurse who 'wants me to go to the hospital,' the doctor 'who wants to see me ASAP,' the MRI that 'took longer than I expected,' the advisor whose registration change 'didn't go through because there was a restriction ... that she didn't catch,' the job that 'messed up my schedule,' the lack of parking 'due to the career fair,' the door that 'will not close so I cannot leave,' the weather that 'is definitely not helping,' the repair man whom 'I am still waiting for,' the sick grandfather and the possible 'last time ... to see [him],' the family emergency 'that I had to go home for,' and the police officer who pulled me over and 'bombarded [me] with traffic tickets'.

These students' absence accounts were also coded as personal, professional or medical (Hong, 2008). Their 98 'medical' excuses had to do with illness (physical or mental) or doctors' appointments of various kinds. Their nine 'professional' excuses included absences due to internship commitments, job interviews, registration complications or meetings with advisors. And finally, their 66 'personal' excuses incorporated the widest variety of issues including 'had to go home' visits, family emergencies, funerals, legal proceedings, vacation trips, weather-related car trouble, accidents, and parking or traffic problems. The following three absence accounts illustrate each of these categories:

'I just vomited so I won't be coming to class today. I will get the homework from someone.' (Medical)

'I'm sorry this is short notice, but I will not be able to attend class today, March 27th. I have a phone interview for a summer internship I applied for at [...]. It was supposed to be after class, but I was just notified it would have to be changed. I apologize and will put the homework assignments in your box. Sorry!' (Professional)

'I didn't make it to class today because this afternoon when i was on my way there it was snowing pretty hard and the windshield wipers on my car weren't working too well. I thought I would make [it] at first, but I didn't want to chance it getting on the expressway. Who would've thought it would snow in April! I'm really sorry, because I know I just missed a couple of classes, but I will be there on Thursday I promise. Please excuse me.' (Personal)

Table 7.3: Explanation Categories of Class Absence Accounts

Explanation Category	Students' E-mails (Present Study)	Technology Class (TC) (Hong, 2008)	Chinese Class (CC) (Hong, 2008)
Personal	38%	37%	15%
Professional	5%	33%	12%
Medical	57%	30%	73%

A comparison of the present findings with those from Hong (2008) points to several similarities and a few important differences (see Table 7.3). First, the most common excuse voluntarily provided by these students was medical-related. Hong's (2008) TC students, native English speakers, pointed most frequently to personal reasons for their absences but many of them, along with the majority of her CC students, including both L1 and L2 speakers of English, also frequently included medical explanations. Given that both TC and CC students were required to seek 'forgiveness' or 'pardon' for their absences (i.e., have them 'excused'), it is understandable that their reasons would often be based on this third category. Since the present students were allowed to miss class 'as needed', it is interesting that the majority of them also pointed to medical issues. Perhaps it is simply the case that most absences are the result of medical circumstances. Or, the fact that students did not point more frequently to other, less serious issues, might also indicate the seriousness with which they take their roles as students and understand their respective teachers' attendance policies. And, in the case of the illustrative 'personal' account provided above, aware that they have already used up their allowed absences, some students' excuses might be better interpreted as 'masquerades in search of grace' (Snyder, Higgins & Stucky, 1983) as they seek special pardon from a teacher who they hope will understand the severity of their individual situations. In such cases, providing detailed accounts when attributing their absences to non-medical issues may seem like the best way to role the proverbial dice.

Personal reasons registered as the second most popular absence explanation in both the present study and the CC context. In the TC setting, though personal reasons were the most frequently cited, the margin of difference between the three categories was very small. Moreover, the number of absence accounts overall in Hong (2008) was very small compared with that of the present study whose participant pool was considerably larger.

Finally, in both the present study and in the CC context, professional reasons were cited least as causes for absences. Given the fact that these students' main priorities were academic rather than professional, this finding is understandable. Perhaps the particular expertise of the TC students resulted in a greater level of involvement on their part to jobs, internships and other professional-related commitments, thus resulting in a higher number of related absences.

The Present Study: Other Repair Work Accounts

> *'I forgot my spanish books at home, therefore I copied another girl's book in order to be prepared for class tomorrow. I wanted to let you know so you are not alarmed when I have only photo copies of and not the real thing. I will be getting my books this weekend, therefore I will not have a problem the rest of the semester.'*

As previously mentioned, in addition to the 197 absence accounts containing excuses and justifications of various types, 53 other RW messages were identified. As illustrated by the student's concern of misunderstanding expressed in the introductory e-mail above, the content of these accounts was often fascinating from a pedagogical perspective but, given the fewer number of RW e-mails categorized as 'other', much less is known about these kinds of student messages. Nevertheless, these accounts were analyzed for the same features as reported in the previous sections on absence account e-mails. Their content was quite varied but in general, these e-mails accounted for an unsubmitted or late assignment, missed exams or quizzes, tardiness (past or anticipated), or missed appointments.

Timing of Other Account E-mails

> *'It's about 9:05am right now- I'm not sure if you'll check this before class. But just in case, I wanted to let you know that my class registration ... is at 10am eastern time, and that I'm going to be a bit late for class. If the quiz is at the end like usual, I most likley won't miss it. See you later.'*

Though this student was aware that his teacher might not see his e-mail in time to explain his late arrival, he offered an explanation prior to committing the actual offense. In these 53 e-mails, students provided accounts of previous (7) or future (46) actions. Only a handful of messages made any mention of the lateness of their e-mail notices but, given that the majority of these accounts were sent prior to the actual offenses, the late notification was often irrelevant.

Use of Apology Formulas in Other Account E-mails

> *'I just got back from the press to get the packet for our class, but they said they didn't have it. I know you had it in class yesterday so I asked the guy 'are you SURE you don't have it because the teacher had it in class?' and he said 'no it's not in yet.' So, I just wanted to let you know that I went and I'm not skipping out on the homework...unless the guy was lying because he didn't know what he was doing. In any event, I apologize that I won't be prepared for class tomorrow and I hope that's ok...see you then!'*

All 53 of these account messages included some kind of explanation or account for student conduct (see Table 7.4). More than half (29) offered repairs but relatively few included expressions of apology (15) or acknowledgments of responsibility (12). As illustrated by the e-mail above, though these messages included a reason for the respective offenses, apology routines were not as common in these account e-mails as they were in students' absence accounts.

Again, as suggested by Meier (1997), distinct RW situations should be studied separately to determine the particular strategies speakers use to engage in repair. In these account e-mails the most common combination of formulas was that of explanation or account of the situation + offer of repair (23 occurrences). The second most common combinations were expression of apology + explanation or account of the situation + offer of repair (7 occurrences) and expression of apology + explanation or account of the situation (7 occurrences).

Table 7.4: Students' Use of Apology Formulas in Students' Account E-mails

Apology Formula	# of Other Account E-mails	# of Absence Account E-mails
Expression of Apology	15 (28%)	100 (51%)
Explanation or Account of Situation	53 (100%)	190 (96%)
Acknowledgment of Responsibility	12 (23%)	17 (9%)
Offer of Repair	29 (55%)	150 (76%)
Promise of Forbearance	5 (9%)	41 (21%)

Other Accounts: Excuses and Justifications

> 'I am writing this email in English just to make sure I explain thoroughly what I need to. This Thursday, the 18th is 'Blackout Day' on campus. I am involved in this day. It is a day on campus to portray the amount of people who are killed due to drunk drivers. I will be wearing a black shirt with numbers that day and cannot speak from 7:30 AM to 8:30 PM that night. Not speaking at all, during class also. I know this is difficult to do in a Spanish Conversation and Composition class but it is only one day and it is a big part of [this] campus. The group leaders said an email was being sent to all the professors regarding this day. I hope it is not a problem. Thank you.'

Within these non-absence account e-mails, 49 (92%) 'excuses' and four (8%) 'justifications' were identified. As with the absence account messages, attempts to justify students' respective offenses were relatively rare (see Table 7.5). The above e-mail illustrates an exception in that the student tried to justify her upcoming lack of oral participation by highlighting the infrequency and importance of 'Blackout Day' on campus. Nevertheless, most of the students' account messages denied responsibility for their offenses for a variety of reasons.

Table 7.5: Account E-mail Percentages of Excuses and Justifications

	Students' Other Accounts	Students' Absence Accounts
Excuse	92%	88%
Justification	8%	9%
Neither	N/A	3%

Other Accounts: Categories

'Hi, how are you? I just wanted to e-mail you about my presentation in class tomorrow. Today I woke up really sick and I just went to the nurse and I have some kind of tonsilitus and a high fever. I am hoping to be feeling better tomorrow, and I will be in class. The only problem is that Scott and I are presenting tomorrow. We have the whole presentation done, with just one small problem. I have no voice! The nurse said it might start coming back tomorrow, but I can't promise that it will. Is there any way we could present on monday? We will hand it in tomorrow, but I want to be able to get a few words in, haha. Let me know. Thank you!!"

These messages were also analyzed in light of the three categories provided by Hong (2008): personal (74%), professional (7%) and medical (19%) reasons. Table 7.6 provides a comparison of these findings with those of the students' absence accounts and the findings from Hong's (2008) TC and CC students.

Table 7.6: Explanation Categories of Other Account E-mails

Explanation Category	Students' Other Accounts (Present Study)	Students' Absence Accounts (Present Study)	Technology Class (TC) (Hong, 2008)	Chinese Class (CC) (Hong, 2008)
Personal	74%	38%	37%	15%
Professional	7%	5%	33%	12%
Medical	19%	57%	30%	73%

Given the individualized nature of the 'other' category, it was not surprising to find a high frequency of personal explanations, especially when compared to the required absence e-mails reported in Hong (2008).

Students' accounts for their offenses were often (in 22 messages) accompanied by a request for the teacher to allow some kind of special arrangement (i.e., a delayed assignment, etc.) or by statements that some might interpret as presumptuous: 'Hope you understand', 'Hope that's okay', or 'Let me know if there's a problem'. These explicit or implied requests were made regardless of the category of the account. For example, in the introductory e-mail above the student's medical account was accompanied by her request to delay a presentation. Another student's personal account (i.e., 'i forgot to hand in my paper yesterday. i didnt see the folder and it slipped my mind. is it possible to put it in your mailbox today?') included his request to hand in the assignment late. Finally, another student's professional account contained the statement 'I might be a little late for our class' with his implied request for permission at the end: 'Hope that's okay'.

Pedagogical Implications and Future Research

Rather than interpreting absence e-mails as mere *excuses*, teachers might find it helpful to view them as *accounts* that attempt to explain students' situations and actions. Students do not always understand or remember the specific details of a given course's attendance policy; nevertheless, these data revealed that they try to account for their situations before, during and after their actual absences. In addition, many acknowledge the 'late notice issues' that relate to their absence e-mails. Thus, teachers should recognize that students who provide absence accounts are, at least at some level, demonstrating awareness of and responsibility for their need to be in class. The inclusion of some type of explanation was an integral feature of this particular speech act but, in contrast, teachers should not expect to find actual expressions of apology in these accounts; in fact, it is possible that apologetic language is considered optional by students who might not perceive absences to be 'offenses' directed toward their teachers but rather decisions for which they themselves are ultimately responsible. Even so, students frequently do seem to think it necessary to account for absences in order to protect their respective images with their teachers. Thus, teachers should consider if and how to respond to these types of messages. The choice not to respond should be made explicit to students, perhaps when outlining the course attendance policy, so as not to raise unnecessary concerns when their absence account message falls into a silent space. Even more effective might be a brief reply that acknowledges the student's e-mail with a reminder of relevant details of the course's attendance policy. Finally, students' statements such as 'Hope this is okay' or, even the more potentially problematic, 'Thanks for understanding', should not be automatically interpreted as presumptuous. Indeed, these types of closings were included in messages meant to explain absences of students well-aware that their course absence limits had not yet been reached. Thus, in actuality, there was nothing to presume and these statements were likely meant to be polite closings rather than rude statements of expectation.

As claimed previously, a student's ultimate success in repairing his or her image depends on the teacher's evaluation of the excuse or justification provided for the offense. Future research could explore teachers' reactions to the three categories of account e-mails or investigate if teachers are more or less likely to positively evaluate e-mail or face-to-face accounts when framed as excuses or as justifications. That is, how do teachers react when students deny or, conversely, accept responsibility while attempting to explain or even reduce the offensive effect(s) of their actions?

In addition, different classroom policies of various types (attendance, late work, etc.) might also influence teachers' evaluations of a student's account. Given that their expectations for student behavior vary considerably, teachers' respective reactions to students' offense explanations are likely to demonstrate an equal or even greater level of variability.

In the specific context of e-mail, the likelihood that a student would tell the teacher that an absence was due to her choice to extend a trip or his decision to attend a ballgame would probably be reduced if the teacher exercised the practice of excusing (or not) each individual absence rather than allowing students to be absent a certain number of times for any reason. Future research on absence-related e-mail accounts should take such variables into consideration.

CHAPTER EIGHT

Expressions of Gratitude

> 'I just wanted to thank you for a great semester. I wanted to wait until after grades were in to write you, because I want you to know how sincere I am in saying this. You are one of the best teachers I've ever had. I felt like I've learned more this semester in Spanish than I have for the past 5 years. Thanks for everything and have a great summer.'

Throughout history, there have been many contexts in which, to be considered polite, thanking was required (Jacobsson, 2002). Though thanking is usually viewed positively, expressing gratitude to teachers can be a complex task for students. Indeed, Okamoto & Robinson (1997) claimed that one's choice of expression is dependent, at least in part, on the relationship between interlocutors. Sent after final course grades had been made official, the above message strategically anticipates and counters the unfortunately common suspicion held by some teachers that students express gratitude and give compliments only to earn undeserved brownie points from the one who assigns their grades. It is regrettable that students who do 'kiss up' to their teachers make it problematic for others to express genuinely positive reactions about their course experiences. Not only do teachers miss out on the encouragement such messages provide, students find interactions with teachers to be more challenging than they should be.

In fact, for students the situation is even more complex than what is described above. Eisenstein & Bodman (1993) found that thankers often articulate initial expressions of gratitude but wait for the receivers to reply before offering more demonstrative forms of thanks. Logically impossible in a single e-mail, this practice illustrates the sometimes competing factors at play when a student wishes to thank a teacher; specifically, the student might feel genuine gratitude for a teacher's action but, simultaneously, recognize the need to balance the intensity of his/her expression of gratitude with the possibility of it being misunderstood or the teacher finding it unacceptable. For example, as mentioned in Chapter 1, a *New York Times* article reported that an English professor advised students to thank their teachers upon receiving responses to the students' previously-sent messages (Glater, 2006). Though some teachers might appreciate this high level attention to e-mail etiquette, others might judge these kinds of thank you e-mails as unnecessary and even undesirable – at best, 'clutter,' and at worst, ingratiating. Thus, even the most sincere intentions are subject to scrutiny and potential misinterpretation.

As documented in Chapter 5 and seen in previous research (Lee & Park, 2011), it is well-known that students frequently use 'thank you' or 'thanks' as sign-offs on messages in which they are making requests. In fact, even before academic e-mail existed, Apte (1974) claimed that these highly frequent expressions of gratitude were sometimes received and interpreted as more mechanical than meaningful. In addition, several researchers (Aijmer, 1996; Eisenstein & Bodman, 1986, 1993; Aston, 1995) emphasized the use of 'thank you' as part of a conversational closer, a function seen in the current study and presented in Chapter 4. The present chapter does not address these common uses of 'thank you'. Rather, its focus is the 68 e-mails used deliberately by students to express gratitude to their teacher for the reasons described in Table 8.1.

Table 8.1: Students' E-mail Thank Yous

Reason for Thank You	Number of E-mails
Providing Registration or Advising Help	13
Sending Homework Assignment or Document	9
Writing a Letter of Recommendation	9
Giving Overall Support as Teacher/Advisor	7
Providing Course Material Help	7
Other/Undeterminable	7
Allowing Rescheduling of an Appointment, Exam, Quiz or Presentation	6
Postponing an Exam, Quiz or Assignment	5
Answering a Grade Question	2
Notifying Student of a Lost Item	2
Granting Permission for a Student to Miss Class for a Special Event	1

The topics of the majority of these thank yous represent areas for which professors are regularly responsible (e.g., registration or advising help, homework assistance, writing a letter of recommendation, etc.). However, students also wrote thank you e-mails to express gratitude for actions that the teacher was not obligated to perform (e.g., rescheduling an exam, postponing an assignment, or notifying a student who had left an item in their classroom).

A considerable amount of research on expressions of gratitude in academic contexts has focused on non-native speaker speech, particularly the pragmatic difficulties they encounter when expressing gratitude in their respective L2s (e.g., Aston,

1995; Cheng, 2010; Eisenstein & Bodman, 1986; Pérez, 2005; and, Schauer & Adolphs, 2006). For pedagogical reasons, Schauer & Adolphs (2006) even recommended that second language students be exposed to samples of native speakers' expressions of gratitude in different contexts by using actual DCT (discourse completion task) or corpora data in the classroom. Specifically, they claimed that students might benefit from the analysis and subsequent imitation of the ways in which native speakers thank interlocuters in both controlled, invented contexts (DCTs) and in real-life interactions (corpora data). The present data, representing naturalistic examples of native speakers' e-mail thank yous, provide such information and, as such, warrant a detailed analysis.

Types of Thanking Expressions

In her study of corpora data, Cheng (2010) divided thanking expressions into six category types: thanking, appreciation, non-gratitude, combinations, thanking a third person, and formal speech. It is important to note that Cheng's (2010) coding was tied to each occurrence of thanking expressions in her data rather than to particular moments in which someone composed a more elaborated thank you. In contrast with her examples, consisting of entirely oral, spontaneous expressions of gratitude, the present data represent a written context in which the interaction was neither face-to-face nor synchronous. As such, these 'speech events' are less spontaneous (i.e., not occurring in real-time) and probably entailed more deliberate thought as the e-mail authors had time to compose and revise their respective messages, sending them only after being satisfied with their particular content. Thus, they are probably more comparable to written 'thank you notes' than oral 'thank you expressions'. Nevertheless, Cheng's (2010) categories (limited to the first four) offered a helpful framework in which to analyze these messages.

Cheng's (2010) first category, 'thanking', included five subtypes: simple thanking (e.g., *thank you, thanks*); elaborated thanking (i.e., thanking and adding one intensifier); more elaborated thanking (i.e., thanking and adding two intensifiers); thanking and stating the reason (e.g. *thanks for ...*); and thanking with intensifier(s) and the reason. For Cheng (2010), the reasons for which one might thank an interlocutor included favors, impositions, and positive feelings. Her second category, 'appreciation', accounted for phrases such as 'I appreciated' and 'It's much appreciated' and was broken down into three types: showing appreciation and adding an intensifier (e.g., *much* or *so*), showing appreciation and stating the reason, and showing appreciation and adding intensifier(s) and the reason. Her third category, 'non-gratitude', included statements that communicated relief (e.g., *thank goodness*), rejected an offer (e.g., *No, thanks anyway*), or showed politeness, greeting and conversation ending (e.g., *Thank you, you too* in response to *Have a nice day*). Finally, her fourth category, 'combination', recognized that thanking expressions often spread across two sentences in which the first sentence actually thanks the other and the second states the reason, or the first thanks the other with an intensifier(s) and the second adds the reason. Cheng's (2010) final two categories (thanking a third person and formal speech) were not relevant to the analysis of the present data.

Given the written nature of these thank yous, it was expected that students would likely spread out their expressions of gratitude over more than one sentence and that, therefore, many instances of the fourth category ('combinations') would be identified. This, however, was not the case. Though many students expressed particular reasons for their gratitude, those reasons were always included in the same sentence as the actual 'thank you', with only one exception. It was also expected that students' reasons would be easily categorized according to the particulars of this educational context applying Cheng's (2010) three-way framework: favors (something unusual the teacher did for them), impositions (the teacher's fulfillment of a request that required significant time or effort), and positive feelings (the students' explicit acknowledgment that the teacher had been particularly kind or understanding). This was also not the case. Even though many students explicitly expressed all of these ideas, the actual reasons they gave (see Table 8.1) for their expressions of thanks were not easily distinguished as favors, impositions or positive feelings. That is, writing a letter of recommendation does require significant time and effort but is not considered by most teachers to be a true 'imposition' unless the request for the letter was made late or under unusual circumstances. When a teacher responds quickly to a student's request for a document that was distributed when he or she was absent, the teacher's effort to send the document is helpful and may arguably be deemed a 'favor', but it is not truly unusual since it falls within what many teachers consider to be their professional responsibilities. In addition, students may call their teachers 'kind', 'understanding', 'patient' and 'helpful', but these positive evaluations are less deserved in a context in which a teacher is merely doing his or her job as opposed to a context in which someone loans money to a friend, puts up with a screaming baby, waits on a fellow diner to finish eating before leaving a restaurant, or tows a stranger's car from a ditch. In short, Cheng's (2010) distinctions are probably most accurate and useful when applied to spoken rather than written real-life data.

The Present Study

Cheng's (2010) broader categories ('thanking', 'appreciation', 'non-gratitude' and 'combinations') were much more easily applied to these data. In these 68 thank you e-mails a total of 134 thanking expressions were identified. The most common student strategies were direct and explicit and, as such, were coded as Cheng's (2010) category one, 'thanking,' (107 occurrences; see Table 8.2). The single most common student strategy (34 occurrences) within category one was to thank the teacher with intensifier(s) and the reason (category one, subtype five). For example, 'Thank you so much for your help. I just got her email now and ...' Following that in frequency (28 occurrences) was to thank the teacher with the reason (category one, subtype four). For example, 'Thank you for your help, but I have decided to stick with things and see what happens.' A relatively close third place (18 occurrences) was to thank the teacher with one intensifier (category one, subtype two). For example, 'Thank you tremendously for the letter.' These results are similar to

Table 8.2. Thanking Expressions by Category (Cheng, 2010)

Category	Subtype	Number of Occurrences	Total
1. Thanking	1. Simple Thanking	12	107
	2. Elaborated Thanking	18	
	3. More Elaborated Thanking	15	
	4. Thanking with Reason	28	
	5. Thanking with Intensifier(s) and Reason	34	
2. Appreciation	1. Appreciation with Intensifier	4	15
	2. Appreciation with Reason	9	
	3. Appreciation with Intensifier(s) and Reason	2	
3. Non-Gratitude	1. Relief Statements	2	3
	2. Rejection of Offer	0	
	3. Politeness, Greeting, Conversation Ending	1	
4. Combinations	1. Thanks. Reason.	0	1
	2. Thanks with Intensifier(s). Reason.	1	
Other	–	8	8
Total		134	

Cheng's (2010) in that she also found the thanking category to be the most common in her data. However, in contrast, she reported simple thanking, 'thank you', to be the most frequently used strategy and that thanking with intensifier(s) and the reason to be among the least frequent.

As in the present study, Schauer & Adolphs (2006) also found that expressions of gratitude with intensifiers occurred more frequently than a simple 'thanks' or 'thank you' alone. In fact, despite the informal nature of e-mail, in this written context of communication, these students were more likely than not to compose their thank yous in complete sentences, including the specific reasons for their gratitude. In all, 122 of these 134 (91%) expressions of gratitude were written with syntax or vocabulary that went beyond simple thanking.

Use of Multiple Thanking Expressions with Reason(s)

'I appreciate your consideration about [extending] the log presentation and the final project date. Thank you for your assistance and have a splendid Thanksgiving.'

As seen in the previous e-mail, it was very common for students to use more than one thanking expression in a single message. In fact, excluding the eight 'Other' instances of thanking expressions that did not fall within Cheng's (2010) categories, in 41 messages (60%) these students used two or more expressions of gratitude (see Table 8.3). The range of thanking expressions per e-mail was from 1 to 6 and the average was approximately 2 per message. Often, the second or final expression was provided near the end of the message or as part of the e-mail's closing as in 'Thank you so much for everything' or 'Thanks again'.

Table 8.3. Frequency of Thanking Expressions per E-mail

# of Thanking Expressions	# of E-mails
1	27
2	29
3	9
4	2
5	0
6	1
Total	68

Not only were multiple thanking expressions frequently included in each e-mail, it was also more common than not for students to include particular thanking expressions that referred to the reason for their gratitude (60% total from category 1, subtypes 4 and 5; category 2, subtypes 2 and 3; and category 4, subtypes 1 and 2) and intensifiers such as 'very', 'sincerely' or 'so much' that strengthened their thanking expressions (60% total from category 1, subtypes 2, 3 and 4; category 2, subtypes 1 and 3; and category 4, subtype 2) .

Other Thanking Strategies: Original Statements and Compliments

> *'Thank you so very much for your glowing recommendation. I truly appreciate your kind words and value your praise immensely. What you have written is above and beyond anything I could ask for. Thank you again, and have a wonderful Thanksgiving break.'*

In addition, as expressed by the statement in the e-mail above, 'What you have written is above and beyond anything I could ask for', there were eight instances in which students made statements that expressed gratitude in original ways that did not fit Cheng's (2010) framework. For instance, to thank their teacher for various actions students used phrases such as the following: 'I am speechless.'; 'Your support really means a lot to me.'; 'I am sincerely grateful for your kind words about me.'; and, 'I really don't know where I would have turned to finish these last (unforeseen!) three credits.'.

Although Coulmas (1981), Cheng (2010), and others have recognized that a thank you can be a response to a compliment, the analysis of these data confirmed Schauer & Adolphs' (2006) finding that a compliment can also be an element of a thank you e-mail. That is, in addition to the strategies listed above, students also provided compliments to the teacher as integral elements of their thank yous in 15 messages. These compliments ranged from professional evaluations of the teacher's pedagogical style to personal comments regarding her character and concern for students. Considering again the possibility for the teacher's misinterpretation of students' compliments or related motivations, their inclusion of compliments is a noteworthy finding. In addition, many of their thank you messages were written with warmth and emotion as conveyed by specific sign-offs such as 'Fondly', students' expressed desires to keep in touch, and hopes to see the teacher in the future.

'Thanks' Versus 'Thank You'

> *'Thank you so much your ideas, they sound great. I'll look into it and hopefully will find enough information. Thanks again and see you tomorrow.'*

Cheng (2010) found that within the subcategory of simple thanking, 'thank you' was used much more frequently than 'thanks'. Some researchers (e.g., Cheng, 2010; Pérez, 2005, and Schauer & Adolphs, 2006) have suggested that differences might be found in thankers' use of 'thanks' versus 'thank you' in various contexts: oral or written, e-mail as compared with conventional letters, or native versus non-native speakers. Given the characteristics of the present data (i.e., written communication produced mostly by native speakers of English in electronic format), these comparisons are beyond the scope of this study. But, this analysis does offer a type of control group with which to explore this feature of e-mail thank yous. Specifically, these 68 messages included the following specific expressions of gratitude (see Table 8.4).

Table 8.4. Occurrences of Expressions of Gratitude

Expressions of Gratitude	# of Occurrences
'Thank You' in a Sentence	44
'Thanks'	25
'Thank You'	22
'Thanks' in a Sentence	17
Form of 'Appreciate'	16
'Grateful' or 'Gratitude'	2

The 44 occurrences of '"Thank You" in a Sentence' included statements that expressed a reason (e.g., 'Thank you for ...') for the student's gratitude. The 25 instances of the single expression 'Thanks' occurred alone or with intensifiers such as 'a lot' or 'very much'. Like 'Thanks', the 22 expressions of 'Thank You' also occurred alone or with intensifiers. The 17 cases of '"Thanks" in a Sentence' also included the reason for the student's gratitude. The 16 occurrences of a 'Form of "Appreciate"' included phrases such as 'I appreciate' and 'I am very appreciative'. And the final two instances within the category, 'Grateful or Gratitude,' included a specific mention of either of those words.

Though the simple 'Thanks' was used slightly more frequently (25 times) than 'Thank You' (22 times), the most frequently used expression of gratitude in these e-mails was '"Thank You" in a Sentence' (44 times). When combined with the occurrences of simple 'Thank You', these two categories accounted for a total of 66 (52%) expressions of gratitude. The simple 'Thanks' and '"Thanks" in a Sentence' categories together accounted for 42 (33%) expressions of gratitude. Thus, overall, instances of 'Thank You' were more frequent than those of 'Thanks'.

Thanking and (Un)Equal Relationships

Though many researchers have focused on the positive effects of thanking, Eisenstein & Bodman (1986) recognized that the failure to express gratitude adequately can have negative social consequences. Based on DCTs, their research found that thankers who felt especially 'indebted, surprised, or overwhelmed' (171) produced a more lengthy thank you than did others. However, they also found that 'shorter thanking episodes sometimes reflected greater social distance between interlocutors' (Eisenstein & Bodman, 1986: 176). Cheng (2010) described these more limited thank yous as 'restrained' or 'unelaborated' (260).

Though contextual variables certainly play a role in the performance and content of speech acts, the present data reveal that these native English speakers' elaborated expressions of gratitude did not seem restrained in spite of the unequal relationships they had with their teacher. In fact, as documented previously, these students' incorporation of multiple thanking expressions, reasons for being grateful, and compliments suggest that in this particular unequal relationship, they may have tried to prevent any possible misunderstanding that could have resulted in their thank you being received as inadequate or ill-formed. In addition to their desire not to be misunderstood, such intentionality on their part might also be explained by whatever sense of indebtedness motivated their respective thank yous in the first place.

Self-Identification

As mentioned in Chapter 2, students' self-identification, or lack thereof, was tracked in the overall analysis. That is, by including statements like 'This is Mary from your Spanish II class on M/W/F at 1:00', some students explicitly identified themselves in their e-mails though other students left it to their teacher to determine who they were by name alone. Along with 0/17 apology and 2/19 complaint messages, the category of thank you e-mails represents the most impressive example (i.e., 0/68); that is, in not even one of these 68 messages did any student include such a self-identification statement. Although many students in both the request and excuse speech act categories self-identified, not one of the students writing thank you messages did so. This finding is not as impressive in the more limited apology and complaint data, but it is noteworthy given the larger number (68) of thank you e-mails.

Apologies, complaints and thank yous are perhaps the most complex, personal messages that students write to a teacher. Requests for a missed homework assignment are not nearly as face threatening as are complaints about a teacher's decision or an apology that accepts responsibility for an offense and seeks restoration. Ironically, a student's excuse about an upcoming absence might be far less potent than a personalized expression of gratitude that could be mistakenly linked to ulterior grade-related motives. Thus, it is possible that students who are comfortable enough to write apology, complaint, and thank you e-mails also are more sure that their teachers know who they are in the first place. For that reason, they may not feel it necessary to identify themselves by course or section number. Likewise, students who compose more 'run-of-the-mill' excuse or request messages may be less certain that their teacher knows who they are individually and, as a result, may be more likely to include such identifying information. Future research might seek more quantitative data to substantiate this hypothesis.

Pedagogical Implications and Future Research

In addition, future research could use the present findings to compare the results of studies based on naturalistic data with those found in more controlled research settings, including DCTs or role-plays. Thank you e-mail features, such as students' use of particular or original expressions of gratitude, incorporation of compliments, or the addition of elaboration, intensifiers and reasons, could vary considerably in these different contexts. Investigating students' thank yous with an elicitation technique (like a DCT) could prove informative; by revealing what students would write in an e-mail without real-world consequences, those elicited data may shed additional light on the naturalistic data presented here.

Other types of studies that explore the assumptions students make regarding how they and their e-mails might be understood by their teachers would be particularly useful for purposes of better understanding and managing student-teacher relationships and interactions. In the meantime, without such information, it would be beneficial for teachers to avoid coming to a rash or unjustified conclusion that a student is expressing gratitude or complimenting a teacher in a disingenuous manner.

Certainly, everyone, both students and teachers, is capable of acting in ways that are insincere for ulterior reasons. Indeed, some university faculty members complain that their colleagues give consistently high but undeserved grades to a limited group of students in order to have at least a small base of student supporters. Of course, it is equally possible that some students praise or thank their teachers only to win their favor with the hopes of receiving positive evaluations of their coursework. However, if a teacher operates with this kind of suspicious mentality and prejudged beliefs it does not support a trusting student-teacher relationship or allow space for students to express sincere gratitude or for the teacher to be encouraged by students' genuine and encouraging affirmations.

Thus, perhaps the most important pedagogical implication of the present findings is for teachers to refrain from negatively presuming that students' expressions of gratitude are insincere and to work to develop learning environments that are mutually beneficial for both students and teachers. Teachers should strive to create honest and safe channels of communication through which they and their students can express gratitude as well as sincere evaluations of each other's performance.

CHAPTER NINE

Complaints

> *'Thank you for your prompt reply, however I was disappointed to hear that you do not feel comfortable writing a letter of recommendation for me. I was not under the impression that it is the policy of X University faculty members to turn away from those who approach them in desperation. Thank you for your time.'*

A cursory look at websites such as RateMyProfessors.com reveals that in such online contexts university students complain most frequently about their grades, the quantity of work assigned, and particularities or idiosyncrasies of individual teachers (pedagogical practices, personal characteristics, and so on). Two explicit categories that students quantify as they evaluate their professors are 'Overall Quality' and 'Easiness' but their descriptive comments often have more to do with their opinions about the helpfulness or likeability of specific professors and whether or not other students should take courses with them. As expected, there is a fairly direct relationship between their complaints and their recommendations.

Definition of a Complaint

One definition of a complaint, loosely built on Olshtain and Weinbach's (1987) framework, is 'an expression of dissatisfaction addressed by an individual A to an individual B concerning behavior on the part of B that A feels is unsatisfactory' (Laforest, 2002: 1596). When A expects something from B (e.g., a specific grade, a letter of recommendation, a certain quantity of homework) that B does not satisfy, A's expectations are violated, resulting in a complaint to B (Olshtain and Weinbach, 1987). The message above clearly communicates a high level of dissatisfaction on the part of the e-mail writer (A) with her former teacher's (B) refusal to respond to her previous request (included below) for a letter of recommendation:

> *'I got your "hello" from [shared acquaintance] and I am happy to hear from you! I hope things are going well for you! I am applying for a job that will require me to use Spanish. To apply for this job, I will need a letter of recommendation from a former professor. I would greatly appreciate if you would provide one of these recommendations. I would be able to come to your office if necessary, or you could fax it to ... [fax number]. This job sounds perfect and I have been unable to find work for 7 months! I desperately need your help! Please accept my deepest gratitude.'*

The student's disappointment and resulting complaint regarding her former teacher's refusal to recommend her was probably prompted in part by her own anxiety over not finding a job for several months. The e-mail she received from the teacher constituted an additional and somewhat unexpected complication:

> '*Thanks for your message. It is good to hear from you. I am sorry that you are having trouble finding work. Since I had you only in one class, I don't feel particularly prepared to write a letter for you. But what about asking [another professor]? I think you have had a lot more contact with her because of your role in [extracurricular activity X]. And didn't you travel with her in [Spanish-speaking country]? She would probably be better able to address your abilities and to evaluate your language ability for a job-like setting. Let me know how things go. I hope you get this job or another one that you like really soon. Sorry I can't be more helpful.*'

House & Kasper (1981) emphasized that by complaining, a speaker communicates the view that what B did (in this case, refuse to write a letter of recommendation) is somehow bad for the speaker. In this situation, the student's dissatisfaction was sparked not by rude communication but by what the student perceived to be an unfair decision. In fact, as Laforest (2002) clarified, B's 'unsatisfactory' behavior is anything that fails to meet A's expectations, in this case, the student's assumption that her former teacher would write the requested letter. Previous studies have found that explicit expressions of disappointment are associated with written complaints (Vásquez, 2011). In this case, rather than reacting just with disappointment or acknowledging the teacher's suggestion to request a letter from a different faculty member in a better position to offer such a recommendation, this student expressed her complaint in a way some might regard as impolite.

Interpretation of a Complaint

Indeed, part of the complexity of complaints, and any potentially face-threatening act (Brown & Levinson, 1987) for that matter, is that the receiver's interpretation of the utterance is likely the most influential element in the interaction. Chen, Chen & Chang (2011) emphasized that many assertions intended to be complaints are interpreted merely as simple comments, and vice versa, many observations intended to be merely comments are mistaken as complaints. Laforest (2002) affirmed this focus on the interpretation of the recipient regarding a complaint as 'anything the speaker said that the hearer took to be an expression of dissatisfaction with his/her behavior' (1597); that is, for research purposes, Laforest depended on the responses of the hearers to distinguish complaints from mere assertions.

Within face-threatening acts, Laforest (2002) pointed out that complaints, disapprovals, criticisms, warnings, and accusations are overlapping and that 'it is not easy (and may not be necessarily that useful) to distinguish very clearly between them' (1597); moreover, in the context of real-life interactions, she asserted that complaints are also hard to distinguish even from requests and excuses. Indeed, student complaints can also be indirectly framed as requests or excuses. And, as pointed out by Vásquez (2011) and Edwards (2005), complaints can be hard to identify since complainers themselves often desire to give the impression that they are not actually complaining when indeed, they are.

Given these complexities, it is unsurprising that many researchers have studied complaints in a variety of L1/L2 settings. For example, through the use of questionnaires, Mulamba (2009) explored the beliefs of speakers of Ciluba, French, and English in regard to complaining and apologizing; he documented similar beliefs among the French and English speakers but found that for Ciluba speakers, social distance and relative power have a greater influence on whether or not these particular speech acts can be performed. Using discourse completion tasks (DCTs), Chen, Chen & Chang (2011) compared American and Chinese complaints and found an overall preference for less-direct complaint strategies. In addition, Tran (2002) explored aspects of pragmatic transfer that affected the realizations of the complaints of Vietnamese L2 speakers of English. And, finally, Hartford & Mahboob (2004) examined complaints in the context of letters written in English to editors of newspapers published in Pakistan and Nepal; they looked specifically at discourse structure and the types of semantic formulas that were used. Overall, they found that complaints preceded requests and were usually delivered directly but mitigated both lexically and syntactically.

Complaints in Naturalistic Settings

A common feature of Laforest's (2002) and Hartford & Mahboob's (2004) research was that both studies were based on naturally-occurring data. That is, Laforest (2002) examined oral complaints and complaint responses in conversations among family members, and Hartford & Mahboob (2004) investigated written complaints from real newspaper readers. Neither data set was elicited by the use of DCTs which ask participants to respond to invented scenarios with complaints that in real-life, they might choose to withhold. Laforest (2002) claimed that even a small data sample, drawn from naturalistic discourse, allows researchers to accomplish the following two tasks (1598–1599):

1. 'to observe complaining in an interactional context that is broader and often more surprising, because the complaints gathered are not dependent on a situation imagined by the analyst in advance'; and,
2. 'to observe the true influence of the constraints related to face management, because the complaints are uttered in a context where things are truly at stake (given that the interactants have a continuing relationship).'

Furthermore, she claimed that this kind of data has 'a better chance of reflecting what people actually do in real life, and is therefore much more trustworthy than artificially elicited pragmatic data' (1599).

The Present Study

The data in the present study come from naturally-occurring e-mail interactions and these student complaints were sent voluntarily in a real-life setting in which the interactants, for the most part, had a continuing relationship. The actual complaint motivators were not 'imagined by the analyst in advance' (Laforest, 2002: 1598), but they were relatively predictable by anyone familiar with student-teacher interactions. Especially given their unequal relationship, students rarely complain directly to teachers about their pedagogical styles or particular actions. Rather, they more commonly report these views on formal course evaluation forms and online sites or share them with fellow students or with faculty supervisors or administrators, especially if situations arise that call for the involvement of less partial outsiders.

Nevertheless, faculty members do receive student complaints, most often after the close of a semester, regarding course grades that were lower than students expected or desired. Murphy & Neu (1996) pointed out that this type of communication is challenging even for native speakers of a language who they claimed 'often pre-plan how they will go about making a complaint' (191). Such pre-planning is certainly the case for students who choose to complain by e-mail rather than in person since they have the opportunity to compose a message and send it only after they have revised it to their satisfaction. Unless students are so upset about the grade they have received or whatever it is that motivated their complaints in the first place that they hastily send angrily-written messages, e-mail writers have the time and space to choose their words carefully, including only and exactly what they truly want to say.

Murphy & Neu (1996) concluded their study of 14 American students' participation in an oral DCT by observing that 'when placed in the position of expressing disapproval to a professor about a grade, American native speakers produce a com-plaint' (209), rather than a criticism. In addition, after presenting these students with the scenario (a teacher who had graded an assignment unfairly), Murphy & Neu (1996) asked the American native speakers of English if they would actu-ally complain to their professor in real life as they had reported in the DCT; they reported affirmative participant responses. But, recognizing that differences might be found, Murphy & Neu (1996) suggested that future studies be carried out in natural settings since students in real life situations with their own professors may be less likely to follow through on these predicted actions, especially face-to-face.

In fact, in the present data, out of 1,403 messages, a total of only 19 complaints were made through e-mail. In addition to the introductory message complaining about the teacher's refusal to write a letter of recommendation, 17 e-mails focused on students' grade-related complaints and one message, framed as representing 'some of [my] classmates', communicated a reportedly collective complaint about the quantity of work due on a particular class day (see Table 9.1).

Table 9.1: Students' E-mail Complaints

	Number of E-mail Complaints
Grade-Related	17
Teacher's Refusal to Write a Letter of Recommendation	1
Quantity of Work Due on Same Day	1

As highlighted by Laforest (2002), distinguishing these e-mail complaints from students' other speech acts, specifically requests and excuses, was quite challenging. Since many of these students often included both requests and excuses to soften or mitigate their complaints, some e-mails were coded as complaints while other fairly similar messages were coded as requests or as repair work (RW) excuses because those seemed to be the primary intentions of the message.

For example, despite the lack of interrogatory punctuation, the following mes-sage was coded as a request for a grade change, rather than an indirect complaint about a grade received:

'I just recieved my grade for your second year Spanish I class and I was hoping that in any way could you check over or do anything to my grade to see if the B- I recieved could be a B. I am only asking this because my G.P.A. is currently a 2.71 and to keep my Merit Scholarship I need a 2.75. So if you could please help me out here I would greatly appreciate it, I dont think I am asking for much here so

if you could please try hard it would be a huge help. Thanks for your time and consideration. Happy New Year.'

Though dissatisfied with his course grade, this student did not express dissatisfaction with the teacher's assignment of his actual grade. Rather, his focus was restorative. He was asking a favor (though he didn't believe he was 'asking for much here'!) and was essentially begging his teacher to 'try hard' to help him, rather than registering a complaint about the grade. In contrast, despite the fact that it also contained a request about a grade, this somewhat similar message was coded as an indirect complaint:

> *'I am really sorry to bother you. I know you told us that you could not tell us our grades over email. But, I saw my grade posted and I wanted to know whether you are permitted to tell me what grade I received on the final. If you can, if you could email me and let me know that would be wonderful. If not, so sorry to inconvenience you. Have a wonderful holiday.'*

Albeit quite polite, behind this student's request for her final exam grade was her dissatisfaction regarding her grade, and perhaps a potential plan to argue her overall course grade on the basis of the exam grade.

Though it might seem arbitrary to an outsider, as the recipient of these messages, the teacher was in the most informed position to determine the communicative intention of each particular e-mail based on her knowledge of the specific characteristics of each situation as well as her familiarity and previous interactions with the students involved. As noted by Laforest (2002) and Chen, Chen & Chang (2011), the interpretation of the hearer or the receiver of a communication carries significant influence as the receiver is ultimately the one who comes to an understanding, accurate or not, of what the speaker intended to convey. Thus, though every intention was made to be objective in the coding of these data, the categorization of these messages was unavoidably interpretive.

In addition to the teacher's own interpretation of these messages, the distinction between request/excuse and complaint e-mails often depended on the timing of the message sent as well as the individual student's reasoning expressed in the e-mail. For instance, e-mails about grades sent prior to a grade being assigned were not interpreted as complaints. However, e-mails sent after a grade was assigned that included statements such as 'I studied very hard' or 'I feel like I worked to my ability' used in support of a request for a grade change were coded as complaints.

Six Realization Patterns of Complaints

Laforest's (2002) research on complaints within family conversations recognized six patterns used by speakers to register complaints with their hearers (the 'complainees') regarding their offensive acts. Specifically, these patterns include the following: (1) alluding to an offensive act; (2) justifying one's discontent; (3) requesting that the complainee justify his/her offensive act; (4) mentioning the offensive act; (5) requesting a change in behavior; and (6) adversely criticizing the hearer (1601). These patterns provide a helpful framework in which to analyze these students' e-mail complaints; thus, each pattern will be examined separately. In the context of these e-mails, except for the two messages regarding: (1) the teacher's refusal to write the letter of recommendation; and (2) the student's complaint concerning the quantity of work that was due, the 'offensive act' in question was always the teacher's assignment of an overall course grade (17 messages).

Laforest (2002) found only two instances when a complaint consisted of two combined patterns so, for her analysis, the patterns were applied in a mutually exclusive way. That is, each complaint instance was categorized as an example of only one pattern. But in the present analysis, complaints were composed and delivered quite differently. Given the written, asynchronous nature of e-mail, a student could easily incorporate one or more of these patterns in the same message. Thus, Laforest's (2002) method for analyzing these e-mail complaints was adapted in the following ways. First, the first and fourth patterns were considered to be mutually-exclusive. That is, each e-mail was searched for any explicit mention of the teacher's offensive act and, if found, the message was categorized as an instance of the fourth pattern. If no explicit mention was made and the student's e-mail only alluded to the offensive act, the message was categorized as an instance of the first pattern. Second, if a message requested that the teacher justify the 'offensive act' in question or requested that the teacher change a 'behavior', the message was categorized as an instance of the third or fifth patterns, respectively, but these patterns were not considered mutually exclusive since a student who sought justification might also request a change. Finally, in the case of the second pattern, multiple instances were occasionally found in one complaint; that is, sometimes more than one statement justifying a student's discontent were included in the same message. Thus, these justification statements were identified and counted throughout all of the e-mails resulting in a greater number of justification statements than overall complaint e-mails. A summary of the results of this analysis is presented in Table 9.2 and summarized below.

Table 9.2: Students' Realization Patterns of Complaints

Pattern of Complaint (Laforest, 2002)	# of Occurrences
1. Allusion to an Offensive Act	18
2. Justification of Discontent	27
3. Request that the ComplaineeJustify His/Her Offensive Act	14
4. Mentioning the Offensive Act	1
5. Requesting a Change in Behavior	5
6. Adverse Criticism of the Hearer	0

First, a speaker might make an allusion to an offensive act without explicitly identifying the act or without accusing the hearer. This kind of statement often takes the form of an assertion that lacks second person markers (e.g., 'you', 'your') and evaluative comments. In only one of these complaint e-mails did a student ever express a complaint directly (e.g., '... I was disappointed to hear that you do not feel comfortable writing a letter of recommendation for me'). The other complaints did not include statements such as 'The grade you assigned is unfair', 'I was surprised by the grade you gave me', or 'I didn't deserve the C- that you posted'. Rather, in all but one of these complaint messages (18), the students never actually mentioned the teacher's 'offensive act' explicitly but alluded to it in the following ways: 'I was just looking at my grade and I was wondering how I dropped down to a C for my final average.'; '... a C+ was a little alarming.'; 'I was concerned when I saw my final grade this morning'; and, 'I just checked my final grades and I was shocked to see that I earned a C+ for linguistics'. Rather than directly accusing the teacher, the students' comments offered positive evaluations of themselves, their own feelings about their grades, and even lexical choices that communicated responsibility for grades they had 'earned.' Rather than using frequent second person markers their messages included multiple uses of first person 'I', 'my', and 'me'.

Second, according to Laforest (2002), speakers might also express their discontent with utterances intended to show that they are justified in protesting the offensive act. In Laforest's (2002) oral data, this played out most frequently in statements expressing how the offensive act affected the complainer; but in the present data, these 27 comments, still centered on the speaker, focused on the reasons they used to justify their grade complaints such as the following: 'I have always been a very good student who received very good grades ...'; 'I felt so sure that I had done very well on my final exam and that it would pull up my average to at least a B– although I was hoping for a B.'; 'I thought I was doing well in the class and I did not think that the final could have brought me down that much.'; 'I feel

I put a very good effort into your class'; 'I studied very hard and I feel like I worked to my ability.'; 'I was just wondering how my final grade came out to be a B+ when all along I had an A?'; 'I know that I was not doing too well during midterms, but I thought my final grade would have been better than a D+'; and, 'I was kinda hoping to get at least a B in the course and thought that I was on track to attain that.'

Third, Laforest (2002) found that speakers often complained by requesting that the complainee justify his or her offensive act. In this context, students' requests were aimed at specific grade details. That is, in 14 messages, they asked the teacher to send them their final exam or paper score, to tell them what they did wrong on the exam or what they could have done better that would have resulted in a better course grade, or, in general, to explain how their overall grade came to be what it was.

As mentioned before, only in the e-mail complaining about the teacher's refusal to write the letter did a student make any comment that explicitly described the offensive act about which they were complaining, Laforest's (2002) fourth pattern. Thus, it was almost non-existent in these data.

According to Laforest's (2002) fifth pattern, speakers might request that the complainee change his or her behavior or make up for the offensive act in some way. In the present data, this pattern surfaced four times when students either asked for a grade change or, in one case, asked for the postponement of at least one assignment due on a particularly busy day.

Finally, in none of these e-mails did students engage in the sixth complaint pattern (adverse criticism of the hearer); that is, they did not intentionally or directly insult the teacher as a means of expressing their complaint. Laforest (2002) found this complaint practice to be somewhat common in her study of family discourse. But, like Chen, Chen & Chang (2011) who pointed out that a potential complainer may avoid complaining if the complainee is 'higher in status or is not very close' (269), Laforest (2002) predicted that this practice would be unlikely among interactants who are not close or who do not share equal status, such as students with their teacher.

An analysis of these patterns suggests that these students did indeed manage complaints as potentially face-threatening acts. As mentioned earlier, in the entire data set, there were only 19 total complaint messages; and, just one explicitly mentioned the teacher's offensive act (refusal to write the letter of recommendation) while the other 18 only alluded to it in various indirect ways. It is interesting to note that the one exception was written by a student who had already graduated from the university and potentially had the least to lose by the expression of her more strongly-worded complaint. Given the unequal status between student and teacher, one would expect students to be less direct and the results are not surprising. In fact, Laforest (2002) reported the opposite findings, a more direct approach to complaining, in a context of equal status; the family member participants in her study explicitly mentioned the offensive act very often (32 times) and alluded to it much less frequently (three times). In the present study, though students might have wanted to complain to their teacher about more mundane issues typical of regular classroom interactions and experiences, they did not, but instead chose to complain only about issues that were of a more serious nature (i.e., mostly grades). Furthermore, though the semester had concluded for all the students who complained about their grades, they were unlikely to express their complaints explicitly, perhaps because they anticipated future contact with their teacher. In fact, two of their messages specifically mentioned that they planned to see the teacher the following semester in a future class or on campus. It is likely that their complaints were worded more indirectly in order to preserve the student-teacher relationship.

Moreover, as a group, these students included 27 different reasons to support the 19 complaints they expressed. This explicit documentation suggests that they felt it necessary, perhaps to mitigate a potential loss of face, to explain the reasons for their complaints rather than merely to complain. Some wanted the teacher to provide documentation; that is, 14/17 students felt free enough to request that their teacher justify the grades they had received by sending them additional information. Some might interpret this request as inappropriate, but many others recognize students' right to know their individual assignment grades and to understand how their overall course grade is calculated.

Mitigated and Intensified Complaints

According to Brown and Levinson (1987), Laforest (2002), and others, the potential for a face-threatening speech act like a complaint to negatively affect the speaker can be either mitigated or, conversely, intensified by a variety of factors. Many of these linguistic features are prosodic in nature and relate to the speaker's tone of voice, volume, intonation, or speed of utterance while others are visually significant like gestures or facial expressions. A complaint delivered in an angry tone is obviously much more face-threatening than one uttered with a playful look. But, given the absence of audio and visual features in written data, these linguistic features play out in other ways.

No evidence was found of the use of intensifiers but the potentially face-threatening nature of these student e-mail complaints was mitigated by a combination of elements such as modals ('could' or 'would'), phrases like 'I was wondering' or 'I was hoping', words such as 'just' or 'really' (also found in Murphy & Neu, 1996), explicitly polite markers such as 'I would appreciate it', 'please,' and 'thank you', as well as expressions of well-wishes for a good vacation or a restful break.

For example, statements requesting specific grade information included the following (italics added to highlight the mitigators mentioned above): '*I was just wondering* what grade I received on the final paper.', '*I was just wondering* so if you *could* let me know, *I would appreciate it*', '*I was just looking* at my grade and *I was wondering* how I dropped down to a C for my final average.', '... a C+ was a little alarming. Although I feel I put a very good effort into your class, *I am wondering* what I could have done better in your class to receive a much better grade. Since I have you for Spanish next semester, your insight will help me greatly. *I hope you are having a great break* and I am looking forward to your class next semester.', 'If my grade was a borderline B- *I would really appreciate it* if you *could* change it for me. *Thanks* for everything this semester. *I hope your holiday is great*.', and '*I was wondering* how I got the D+. Did I do horrible on the final because I thought the quizzes averaged out to a C+ and A for the presentation, did all the homework and missed only one class (the one before thanksgiving, had a train to catch). I was *just* surprised by that grade, *thanks*.'.

Another mitigation technique, as explained by Murphy & Neu (1996), is the depersonalization of the issue or problem addressed; this type of framing is another way to mitigate the potential damage brought on a speaker who complains. Their DCT participants used subjects such as 'the paper', 'it', 'the grade' rather than the person (i.e., 'you') to transfer blame from the professor to the problem thus reducing the accusatory nature of their complaints. Or, as they also pointed out, another technique was for participants to accept partial responsibility for a situation with phrases such as 'I know that a lot of the problems [in the paper you evaluated negatively] are mine' or 'I'm wondering whether it was just lack of explanation on my part of if you had overlooked a few things which I had presented'. In the present data, including the example statements in the previous paragraph, many students employed the second technique and accepted at least some responsibility for their situations with phrases such as '[the] grade I received', 'I dropped down', 'what I could have done better', and 'did I do horrible...?'.

Complaints and Arguments

In her investigation of close family member interactions, Laforest (2002) found that her participants' complaints rarely resulted in serious arguments. By its very nature, an argument is characterized by multiple turns on the part of interlocutors who each express opinions and disagreements over the issue in question. Despite (or perhaps, because of) the greater social distance between these students and their teacher, neither did these students' complaints lead to considerable disputes, except to a certain degree in the case of the student who wanted a letter of recommendation. The disappointment and probable indignation she felt over her former teacher's response changed the friendly tone in which she wrote her first message requesting the recommendation to the provoked, sarcastic tone of her second. Her first e-mail included positive expressions such as 'happy to hear from you', 'greatly appreciate', and 'deepest gratitude', polite markers like 'would', 'could', and 'please', along with a generous use of exclamation points. Her second e-mail, though opened and closed with 'thank you' statements, included negative expressions such as 'disappointed to hear', 'I was not under the impression', and 'you do not feel comfortable' along with her possibly sarcastic reference to the existence of a university policy that faculty 'turn away' from students requesting help. A quick read of her complaint might result only in offense, especially considering that her somewhat aggressive tone could not be traced to a rude response from the teacher.

The subsequent exchange, given its peaceful conclusion, could not be characterized accurately as an argument, but it did consist of additional turns on the part of the interlocutors. The teacher responded to the student's complaint by explicitly negating the existence of any such 'policy' and explaining, from her perspective, how students typically go about the process of requesting letters, especially when choosing a potential recommender. She also pointed out why it would be to the student's benefit to select a different professor and implied that supplying the teacher with relevant information (job description, etc.) would be useful. In her initial request e-mail, the student had used a phrase containing a lexical item (i.e., 'I desperately need your help') that she repeated in her complaint message (i.e., she claimed that she approached the teacher 'in desperation'). So, finally, the teacher returned to the notion of 'desperation' and expressed that in this situation, she did not believe she was able to be helpful to the student though, in theory, she would have been willing. Her e-mail was as follows:

> *'There is no set 'policy'. In my experience, students request letters of recommendation from faculty members in whose classes they received very high grades and whom they got to know extremely well over the course of one or more semesters. Since we only had 1 class together and your course grade was a B+, it is in your best interest to request a letter from a professor who can positively evaluate in more detail the strengths that you would bring to this position (whatever this position is: you didn't send me a description or any information regarding the job). Certainly, you never need to approach me with 'desperation'. If I believed that I could be helpful to you in this process, I would be happy to do so.'*

Judging by her following response, the student seemed to have accepted this explanation and responded once again in a respectful tone, both with expressions of gratitude and a declaration of her intent to follow through with the teacher's original suggestion:

> *'Thank you for considering my request and I appreciate your point of view. I will follow your advice and seek recommendations from professors with whom I had more contact during my time at X University. Thank you for your time.'*

Pedagogical Implications and Future Research

These students' complaints were often expressed indirectly (as in Chen, Chen & Chang, 2011) and they were mitigated in various ways (as in Hartford & Mahboob, 2004). When instructed to express disapproval about a grade, Murphy & Neu's (1996) student participants did so but, like the students in this real-life context, they used several complaint techniques including alluding to the problematic issue rather than addressing it directly. As claimed by Laforest (2002), these natural data are more likely to reflect what students actually do in these particular scenarios because, first, the situations were not imagined by a researcher ahead of time and, second, the students faced real consequences for their decisions and words in their ongoing relationship with the teacher.

There is much research to be done to better understand student complaints, but the challenges for empirical investigations are many. First, given the high stakes at risk when students complain to their professors, actual complaints are relatively infrequent, especially when compared to those that take place in other social contexts (e.g., restaurants, hotels, online customer feedback sites, etc.). Moreover, student complaints are often framed as requests for information or for help of various kinds thus, it is even possible for them to go unrecognized by the teachers who receive them. In addition, some students complain in person, directly or indirectly about problematic situations; capturing those kinds of oral interactions for research purposes is plagued with multiple ethical and practical challenges.

However limited might be the results from role-play and DCT studies, those investigations can shed light on the structure of complaints. In addition, other studies could be focused on determining whether and in what circumstances students themselves claim that they do or would complain to their own teachers in real-life settings.

Even from what little is known about student complaints, there are several implications for teachers. First, it is quite possible that the number of complaints teachers receive varies considerably. One can easily imagine that factors such as subject matter or difficulty, individual teaching style or personality, or even university or grading policies would influence, positively or negatively, the likelihood for students to complain and, in turn, the number and types of complaints a particular teacher receives. It is quite possible that healthy student-teacher relationships play a part as well, both in the complaints themselves as well as in their potential to be resolved effectively. Thus, teachers should evaluate their own situations and experiences and determine for themselves the degree to which they or their actions might increase student complaints. Certainly, any context in which one person evaluates another has the potential for ill will and negative interactions. But, there is much a teacher can do to set up policies and procedures in ways that foster security on the part of students and a mutual understanding about the expectations for each other's behavior. Transparent grading rubrics, clear assignment instructions, and well-documented course policies are effective methods for reducing tensions and minimizing the potential for misunderstandings.

Also, the case of the student unhappy about her denied request for a recommendation emphasizes that teachers can indeed respond to at least some complaints in ways that preserve the relationship as well as help students learn to evaluate situations based on criteria that might have been outside their own previous experiences. Rather than instantly taking complaints personally, teachers can often benefit from considering situations from the student's perspective before responding. A careful reading of (or listening to) a student's complaint might reveal the actual reasons for which the student is complaining; these may include fears about finding a job, anxiety over an increasing workload, or concern about a scholarship riding on a particular GPA that is at risk. The need for academic rigor and a teacher's decision to recommend a student are, of course, independent of the potential for students to complain about denying their recommendation requests, assigning appropriate coursework, or determining their grades. But, recognizing and understanding common complaint motivators can be useful in responding to them effectively.

Part of adult socialization is learning if, when, and how to register one's negative personal reaction to an action of another. Such complaining is a complex endeavor that, in many professional and social contexts, carries serious consequences. These particular students' complaints were remarkably polite. They alluded to problematic issues rather than personalizing the situations or aggressively criticizing or accusing their teacher. They often explicitly explained why they were concerned enough about the issue to raise the complaint in the first place. And, most of their requests for the teacher to change the situation were crafted politely and respectfully. Thus, at least in this context if not in others, their complaints deserved equally respectful attention on the part of their teacher.

CHAPTER TEN

Student Use of L1/L2

Hola Professora, [Hello, Professor]

Yo espero que tu tienes un buen vacacion. * [I hope that you have a good vacation.]
Well that is my spanish for the day, anyway I was wondering if you could e-mail
me what I got on the spanish test because I just want to assess where I am at in
your course. There is no rush so even if you don't want to do it, it is fine, but if you
could I would really appreciate it. Sincerely Yours, [Student Name]

Methodological debates over the exclusive use of the target language in L2 pedagogy have prompted numerous studies of the role of the L1 and L2 in language
classrooms. Excessive L1 use has been consistently discouraged (Chambers, 1991;
Duff & Polio, 1990; Polio & Duff, 1994; Turnbull, 2001), and, though a growing
number of researchers (Antón & DiCamilla, 1998; Cook, 2001; 2005; Edstrom,
2004; 2006; 2007; 2009; Macaro, 2005; Storch & Wigglesworth, 2003; Swain
& Lapkin, 2000) affirm its important role in specific contexts, there is continued
emphasis on nearly exclusive target language interaction among L2 teachers and
learners.

The degree to which this expectation extends beyond classroom walls is
unknown. On one hand, some teachers claim to interact predominantly in the L2
with students, even during office hours and on e-mail. In addition to L2 e-mail,
those who favor extending students' use of the L2 outside of the classroom often
integrate discussion boards, online chats, blogs, and even live, personal L2 interaction in electronic forums such as Skype and Twitter. On the other hand, other
teachers view out-of-class communication as an appropriate, and perhaps necessary,
site for L1 exchanges. Some allow L1 interaction outside of the classroom if indeed
the teachers speak their students' L1(s). In such cases, students may talk to them
in the L1 about issues such as homework assignments, grammar questions, course
advising, career planning, personal situations, medical problems, etc. In fact, some
teachers who enforce an L2-only policy in class may even encourage language students to visit them outside of class if they need extra help in their L1. In many ESL/
EFL contexts, the English teacher may not share the native language(s) of all of his
or her students and the question of L1 use in student-teacher interaction becomes
a moot point altogether. Nevertheless, in the case of a Spanish teacher, for example,

(*Students' grammatical errors are not all specifically identified in this chapter.)

in any K-16 context within the United States, it is quite probable that the teacher also speaks English. Provided that his/her students speak English (an assumption that could be unfounded in some educational contexts), the possibility exists for the teacher and students to interact in Spanish (the target language or L2) or in English (the probable L1 or native language of the majority of the students).

Interestingly, few studies have systematically analyzed the language used in student-teacher communication outside the classroom. The present analysis focuses on the language that students chose to use in their e-mails and examines the specific communicative contexts in which they opted for the L2. Though students opted for the L2 much less often than the L1, they did use it in a variety of communicative contexts.

E-Mail as a Pedagogical Tool

Many researchers have emphasized the pedagogical role that e-mail can play. For example, Molina Garrido (2000) used e-mail in the context of a writing activity. The students carried out written role plays in their L2. Strenski, Feagin, & Singer (2005) highlighted the ability of e-mail to facilitate small group peer review. Anderson (2002) promoted e-mail tutoring in an online writing lab and Rose (2004) studied autobiographical e-mail epistolaries. Biesenbach-Lucas & Weasenforth (2002) and Atamian & DeMoville (1998) pointed to e-mail's importance in creating virtual office hours. Worrells (2001) acknowledged its utility for students to submit their course work by attachment. Specifically related to L2 teaching, Pérez (2000), O'Dowd (2003), and Itakura (2004) encouraged the use of e-mail as a site for cross-cultural penpals.

Spanish Language Experience

Before analyzing these students' L2 use (Spanish), it is important to review their Spanish language experience (see Chapter 2 for detailed information). Their exposure to Spanish outside the classroom is unknown but these 338 students were enrolled in one Introduction to Linguistics class (45 students), taught in English, and/or various levels of university Spanish classes (293 students), taught primarily in Spanish, ranging from beginning (42 students) and intermediate-level language courses (90 students), to upper-level Spanish courses designed primarily for majors and minors (161 students). Thus, the students' Spanish language ability ranged from zero to more advanced levels of proficiency. In total, the students enrolled in Spanish courses authored approximately 85% of all e-mails included in this study while students enrolled in the Linguistics course (most of whom did not speak any Spanish) authored approximately 15% of the messages. Regardless, very few e-mails (63, or 4.5% of the total e-mails included) were written entirely in Spanish and most by upper-level students.

Spanish/English E-Mails

Of the remaining 1,340 messages not written entirely in Spanish, the large majority (over 70% of the total e-mails included in the study) were composed entirely in English. The rest of the e-mails were written in a combination of Spanish and English; that is, when one Spanish word was included in an e-mail (including just an 'Hola,' 'Gracias,' 'Profesora,' ('Hello,' 'Thank you,' 'Professor,'), etc.), the e-mail was not counted as having been written 'entirely in English'. In fact, the large majority of these mostly English or 'Spanish/English messages' were written in English with very limited use of Spanish. For example:

> Profesora, *[Professor,]*
> *I was a little dazed after the mid-term and was in a rush to get to my next class and I forgot to copy the homework from the board. I would really appreciate it if you could send the assignment to me. My apologies.* Gracias, *[Thank you,]*
> *[Student Name]*

This Spanish/English e-mail illustrates one of the students' most common uses of Spanish, sprinkling it in as (part of) an opening, term of address, or closing. Students also used Spanish words to refer to a course assignment (e.g., 'I'm attaching my Observacion (Observation))'; as a subject line for an e-mail (e.g., tarea, clase, pregunta, muchos problemas (homework, class, question, many problems)); as a random word or short phrase (e.g., I apologize for missing class today. Hoy ha sido el peor día. (Today has been the worst day.) I was late going to class from work and got pulled over.); as part of a grammar question (e.g., 'Should I change it to 'las catedrales'? (the cathedrals)'); and to refer to themselves by a chosen Spanish name (e.g., José, Marielena, Esteban).

Thus, though these messages were not categorized as 'Only English,' there was very little Spanish in them and most contained only single Spanish words or very short phrases. In fact, it seemed that when most students wanted to express their reason for e-mailing, even when they incorporated some Spanish, they chose to use their L1 for describing getting pulled over by the police officer, requesting exam grade information, or carrying out whatever communicative function motivated their e-mail in the first place.

'Only Spanish' Messages

As previously mentioned, 63/1403 (4.5%) e-mails were written entirely in Spanish. These messages underwent a detailed analysis to determine who wrote them and the message function (e.g., request, excuse, etc.). A couple of these students also tried to express humor while using Spanish. Finally, a few e-mails served as a small window through which it is possible to view at least some students' perspectives on their use of Spanish and/or English in e-mails to their teacher.

'Only Spanish' E-Mail Authors

Dear Profesora,	[Dear Professor,]
Lo siento! Aqui esta mi letra.	[I'm sorry! Here is my letter.]
Eduardo	[Edward]

It was revealing to identify the characteristics of those students who chose to compose 'Only Spanish' messages. There were only two: The brief e-mail above, containing a false cognate ('letra'), was composed by a student in beginning Spanish; the other 'Only Spanish' e-mail sent by a beginning Spanish student contained his short homework composition, written entirely in Spanish, but no other text. Thus, only two beginning-level students wrote e-mails entirely in Spanish (ignoring the one word 'Dear' in Edward's e-mail above). Intermediate-level students accounted for only three messages and the rest (58) were written by upper-level Spanish students, including 15 e-mails by a Latin American student (a Spanish learner and fluent speaker of Portuguese) and 10 by one other upper-level Spanish student (a very highly-motivated Spanish learner and native English speaker) (see Table 10.1).

Table 10.1: 'Only Spanish' E-Mail Author Characteristics

Spanish Course Level	# of e-mails containing at least one occurrence
Beginning	2 (3%)
Intermediate	3 (5%)
Upper-level	58 (92%)
Total	63 (100%)

It is likely that the two students whose 'Only Spanish' messages represented almost half (25) of the upper-level sample (58) had personal reasons for choosing to write in Spanish. Interestingly, they (and a few others) sent 'Only Spanish' messages even in response to messages composed by the teacher in English regarding issues such as a complicated homework assignment or a cancelled class.

In total, 13 students, each writing between two and 15 messages, wrote 50 of these 'Only Spanish' e-mails (79% of the entire set); the remaining 13 messages (21%) were written by 13 different students, each writing only one of these messages. Thus, a total of 26 students composed the entire set of 63 'Only Spanish' e-mails (see Table 10.2).

Table 10.2: 'Only Spanish' E-Mail Authors

	# of Student Authors	# of E-Mails Written by Each Student
	1	15
	1	10
	3	3
	8	2
	13	1
Total	26	63

Communicative Functions of 'Only Spanish' E-Mails

Like all messages included in the present analysis, 'Only Spanish' e-mails were sent for a variety of reasons (see Table 10.3). However, some interesting similarities and differences can be seen by comparing the analysis of 'Only Spanish' e-mails with the overall analysis of the rest of the 1,340 e-mails that made up the entire data set.

Table 10.3: E-Mail Functions

Function	Written in 'Only Spanish' E-Mails (% of total functions)	Written in 'Only English' and 'Spanish / English E-mails (% of total functions)
Requests	28 (42%)	828 (59%)
Excuses	7 (11%)	250 (18%)
Thank Yous	4 (6%)	68 (5%)
Apologies	1 (2%)	17 (1%)
Complaints	0 (0%)	19 (1%)
Dropbox	14 (21%)	78 (6%)
Other	12 (18%)	155 (11%)
Total Functions	66*	1415

(* The number of total functions does not equal the number of total messages because some messages contained more than one type of function.)

In terms of overall frequency, clear similarities exist in the areas of requests, excuses, thank yous, and apologies with requests being only slightly more common in English messages than in 'Only Spanish' messages. Thus, the analysis of these data showed little to no preference for students writing only in Spanish or in English (or Spanish / English) to carry out these four functions. It is important to note that the numbers are somewhat inflated since 161 messages accounted for above were composed by students enrolled in Introduction to Linguistics and most of these students did not speak Spanish and were therefore unable to choose to write in Spanish. It is equally important to note that the 'Only Spanish' e-mail data were a very small set, composed by a limited number of students. A larger number of e-mails might have resulted in very different overall percentages.

However, two important differences were noted when comparing the analyses of both sets of data. The students did not choose to compose even one complaint entirely in Spanish. And, 'Only Spanish' messages were more frequently used for the dropbox function. This is understandable since it would be harder for a language student to complain, a complicated high-stakes pragmatic function, in their L2 and easier to use their L2 to electronically submit a homework document, an action typically requiring very little accompanying text. Indeed, Edward, the Beginning Spanish student mentioned earlier, was able to use 'Only Spanish' in his dropbox e-mail included above.

The largest percentage of 'Only Spanish' e-mails were requests. A brief case study of e-mails from one student reveals several interesting issues. Here is one of her request messages:

> Profesora,
> No entiendo la tarea en el paquete en la pagina 9, no puedo encontrar algunas palabras 3, 4, 5, y 8.
> [Student Name]

> Professor,
> I don't understand the homework in the packet on page 9, I can't find some words 3, 4, 5, and 8.
> [Student Name]

This straight-forward request for homework help is not accompanied by any politeness markers (besides an academic title as a form of address). It might be that this particular student's e-mail style is relatively simple and brief and that her e-mails typically lack politeness markers. She did not write other simple request e-mails in English but she did write one Spanish/English message that contained a request as part of an absence excuse. It was as follows:

> Hi Dr. [Teacher Name],
> I'm sorry but *I will not be able to make it to class today, hopefully I will be able to stop* by during your office hours *to see what I missed and* I will get notes from someone. *If you* wouldn't *mind could you* please *give my e-mail and my cell phone out to the two girls with whom I am doing comparacion de adjetivos. My email is this, xxx and my cell phone is xxx,* thank you!
> [Student Name]

The differences are noticeable. Her absence excuse contains many of the features associated with politeness including an apology and two offers to remediate the situation. The accompanying request, that the teacher give her contact information to her group mates, will benefit her but will also help her classmates who would otherwise be unable to contact her to complete their collaborative assignment. Her request contains a modal, a 'please,' and the message closes with an expression of gratitude.

Comparisons of the two e-mails should not be overstated since the first does not contain an absence excuse and is much less involved. However, the request in the second e-mail contains three different politeness markers, all of which are absent from her first request written entirely in Spanish. It is possible that she was frustrated by not understanding the homework and hastily composed the 'Only Spanish' e-mail without giving thought to politeness strategies. But, given that her e-mail did not communicate even a hint of homework panic or stress, as an upper-level student of Spanish, she likely lacked the pragmatic ability or awareness to incorporate extensive politeness markers in Spanish. Moreover, it is likely significant that she chose to write the first message in Spanish but the second mostly in English; this decision may reflect her own awareness that her level of Spanish proficiency enabled her to communicate a simple request for homework help but not the potential threat to face of an absence excuse in her L2.

This interpretation was confirmed by another of the same student's brief 'Only Spanish' e-mails. It was categorized as 'Other' because it was written entirely in response to a reminder e-mail from her teacher to stop by and fill out an advising form that required her signature:

> Hola Dr. [Last Name]:
> Bueno, vendre a su oficina este lunes que viene, antes de a la una [sic].
> Gracias,
> [Student Name]

> Hello Dr. [Last Name]
> Well, I will come to your office this coming Monday, before at one o'clock [sic].
> Thank you,
> [Student Name]

Though not a request, this e-mail closed with a polite expression of gratitude. Interestingly, the student chose to respond entirely in Spanish despite the fact that the teacher's reminder was written entirely in English. Thus, it seems that when the student felt that her Spanish proficiency could support the communicative task she wanted to achieve, she wrote in her L2, but she chose to write in her L1 when the stakes were higher and (possibly) beyond her linguistic ability or at least confidence.

That is not to say that all students avoided writing 'Only Spanish' e-mails in more complex situations. For example,

> Profesora [Last Name],
> Lo siento acerca de mis tarea. Yo se no hizo muy bien, pero dos amigos mios murio el viernes en un accidente de coche y ha sido muy duro para mi concentrar en deberes. Mi tarea sera muy bien en el tiempo proximo.

Professor [Last Name],
I am sorry about my homework. I know that I didn't do very well, but two friends of mine died Friday in a car accident and it has been really hard for me to concentrate on tasks. My homework will be very good the next time.

This message was composed by an intermediate-level student who took on the challenge of apologizing to her teacher for the quality of her work, assuring improved future performance, and explaining not only what happened but also the negative effects of a tragic event on her ability to concentrate in an academic environment. Due to its grammatical issues, the message consists of language that might not be fully understood by native Spanish speakers who are not accustomed to interacting with language learners. Nevertheless, it represents a brave attempt on the part of a lower-level student to use her L2 to communicate a relatively complicated message.

Thus, students of different levels made very personal choices regarding the language(s) in which to compose e-mails. Their decisions seemed to depend in part on their own level of proficiency and the complexity of the communicative function.

Humor in 'Only Spanish' E-Mails

Even in 'Only Spanish' e-mails, two students, both upper-level, tried to be funny as they played with their L2. This student's message confirmed a presentation date received from her teacher:

Lo siento!!! Estoy muy confundido porque hay muchas muchas cosas en mi cabeza. Haha. Si, nuestra presentacion es jueves. Muchas gracias!
[Student Name]

I'm sorry!!! I am very confused because there are many many things in my head. Haha. Yes, our presentation is Thursday. Thanks a lot!
[Student Name]

Though not particularly funny, the description of her confusion was meant to be humorous, an intention confirmed by her inclusion of 'Haha,' written in English because she probably did not know the Spanish 'Jaja' equivalent! Another student played with Spanish but in a semantically different way:

Profesora [Last Name],
Lo siento otra vez. Mi impresora no funciona hoy (y creo todos dias). Aqui es mi tarea (En Mi Opinion #1). Nos vemos pronto.
[Student Name]

Professor [Last Name],
I'm sorry again. My printer isn't working today (and I think every day). Here is
my homework (En Mi Opinion #1). See you soon.
[Student Name]

This student's humorous intention is not marked by a 'haha' but her parenthetical comment '(and I think every day)' nonetheless represents a playful use of the L2. Contrasting 'today' with 'every day' juxtaposes the meaning of these adverbial expressions as well as references the many past technological problems this student had experienced in recent weeks, problems about which the teacher was already aware due to previous e-mail correspondence.

Student Perspectives on L1/L2 in E-Mail

A few students explicitly mentioned their choice of e-mail language in their actual messages sent to their teacher. One student offers what can be characterized as a very logical explanation of her choice to write in her L1:

Hello Senora [Last Name],
I am writing this email in English just to make sure I explain thoroughly what
I need to.

Her message went on to explain that she had chosen to participate in a special annual event on campus that recognizes the number of people regularly killed by drunk driving. As part of the day, students, wearing black t-shirts to statistically represent the problem, take a vow not to speak. Their communicative 'absence' is meant to represent those who have been lost and raise awareness. Since this student would be attending a small Spanish conversation class, she felt it necessary to explain her silence ahead of time and be sure that her teacher was aware of the event and the required vow. She expressed her hope that this would not be a problem. Her e-mail was, to some extent, a sort of absence excuse.

Given the importance of this event and the complicated nature of her description that exceeded her lexical and grammatical abilities, this student's explanation of her choice to write in English was reasonable. As an upper-level student, she was capable of communicating the general idea of her message but concern that her teacher fully understand and accommodate the upcoming event with no negative effect on her participation grade or her social face likely prompted her to write in English.

Two other students' e-mails did not provide explicit explanations of their L1 language choice but their comments revealed an interesting perspective. Both of the following students started off their messages by offering apologies for writing in English:

> *Hola, Dra [Last Name], (Hello Dr [Last Name])*
> *Please forgive me for writing this in English, but I have a quick question. ...*

> *Hello Ms. [Last Name],*
> *Sorry this isn't written in spanish!! I just found out today that my poppop is in the hospital as of last night. I will be going home...*

The first message, a request, started off with a Spanish greeting and form of address but immediately changed to English. The second message, an absence excuse, contained only English. What is most interesting is that the students' apologies suggested that they perceived some kind of expectation to write in Spanish, even though there was no such requirement stated or implied by anything the teacher had said in class or included on the syllabus. It is possible that these students had prior experiences with other Spanish teachers that motivated them to apologize for their L1 use. Maybe they thought that by writing in English they were somehow forfeiting 'extra credit' or 'brownie points' that could be earned by demonstrating their commitment to Spanish by using it outside of class. Either way, their apologies suggest that some students seem to think that it is a language teacher's expectation, or at least preference, that students use their L2 in e-mail.

Pedagogical Implications and Future Research

Together these findings highlight the importance of language choice in learners' e-mails and have several implications for L2 pedagogy. While some research supports the efficacy of using e-mail to improve language students' L2 writing proficiency in some pedagogical contexts, student choice should not be ignored. This large set of e-mail data gives a clear picture of students' overall language preference when e-mailing their teacher. That is not to say that students should not be allowed to write e-mails to their teacher (or others) in their L2. In fact, for L2 writing practice, penpals, and other purposes, e-mail may serve as an acceptable, and even ideal, alternative to paper-and-pencil or word-processed L2 writing activities. However, most of these students chose to use their L1 to make requests, complain, apologize, make excuses, and express their gratitude. Though students might be able to carry out these functions in their L2, when given the option, most of these chose to do so in their L1. Thus, teachers should consider allowing for students' preference in e-mail language.

It is not known how these data might have been different if the teacher's L1 were Spanish rather than English. Perhaps the students would have made different decisions. But, these students' overwhelming decision to write their e-mails in the L1 suggests that, at least in this context, they preferred that option. Future studies could examine what effect, if any, the teacher's native language has on students' behaviors and expressed preferences.

It is clear that requiring language students to conduct all e-mail interactions with their teacher in their L2 would be impossible and would certainly discourage, and probably halt, communication, especially from beginning-level students. For instance, how could a Spanish 101 student apologize effectively (and confidently!) to a teacher, explain an absence, or even make a relatively simple request? Perhaps the best solution is the maxim from long ago: *Everything in moderation*. Students could be encouraged (but not required) to use Spanish as much as possible in their e-mail communication with their teacher, but their teacher should be sensitive to the unequal status of the relationship at play and simultaneously assure students that e-mails in English are perfectly acceptable and will not count against them or their grade in any way. Rather than insisting on L1 communication by e-mail, teachers who desire that students practice writing e-mails in the L2 could design creative activities that accomplish that goal outside of regular and necessary communication. For instance, in the same way that some language teachers require students to call and leave a voicemail in their L2 for some communicative purpose, language teachers could design similar activities for the e-mail context without removing the opportunity for L1 student-teacher communication.

Those e-mails that are written in Spanish may provide language teachers with a great deal of information regarding their students' linguistic needs in the areas of grammar, vocabulary, and spelling. In addition, they also reveal students' pragmatic abilities (or lack thereof) and provide teachers with real-life interactions through which they can assess their students' needs. These experiences might prompt related classroom activities (e.g., write an e-mail to your roommate to apologize for not having washed the dishes; write an e-mail to a restaurant owner to complain about the food; write an e-mail to your teacher request an appointment). These opportunities could highlight specific aspects of L2 grammar and vocabulary that are problematic as well as challenging issues more closely related to L2 politeness.

Finally, teachers should obviously be tolerant of students' attempts to use their L2 in e-mail. Grammatical errors, stylistic features, lack of appropriate L2 register markers, and informal tone should be taken in stride by teachers who want to encourage students to attempt genuine L2 communication.

CHAPTER ELEVEN

A few final thoughts: Where to go from here

The present study explored e-mails from one particular group of students communicating with one teacher in one university setting. Certainly other studies might broaden the scope of this investigation by including e-mails written to multiple teachers. Though the overall number of student participants and e-mails was relatively high in this investigation, the students all studied the same language (Spanish) or linguistics. E-mail communication norms of this particular university and student body could certainly limit the generalizability of the present findings. Nevertheless, it was not a goal of this investigation to produce findings that are necessarily relevant in any other context, present or future, but rather to analyze these students' e-mails using a variety of frameworks to determine what characteristics typified their interaction and how their communication strategies compared to those identified in previous studies.

Each of the preceding chapters offered its own conclusions regarding each chapter's respective topic(s). Teachers have been encouraged to see e-mail 'norms' from students' perspectives, to be sensitive and open to personal – and perhaps generational – differences in e-mail style, and to identify various elements that characterize students' e-mail requests, apologies, excuses, expressions of gratitude, and complaints. This final section provides a brief look toward the future of electronic student-teacher communication and a few ideas regarding where researchers might go from here to better understand and appreciate student-teacher interaction.

Better understanding how students communicate with teachers in any context, including classroom interactions, office visits, and electronic exchanges including e-mail, is of the utmost importance to any teacher or researcher who wants to improve it. Caring for students as 'whole people' (Noddings, 2005) feeds a relationship in which learning can take place most effectively. A teacher who feels offended by students' use of emoticons and abbreviated language or by their lack of capitalizations and salutations is poorly positioned to build trust and mutually beneficial interactions. Recognizing particular aspects that typify much student e-mail communication might help some teachers step over what could otherwise strike them as rude or even disrespectful. Moreover, an awareness of how students approach communicative acts such as request-making, expressing gratitude, complaining, excuse-writing, and apologizing could certainly lead to better overall interactions and, in turn, learning environments.

E-mail communication, once considered 'cutting edge' technology, still represents the preferred and most frequent mode of electronic student-teacher communication (Porath, 2011). However, it is likely that other 'e-modes' of communication will eventually replace it. Indeed, many teachers already text regularly with their students and are encouraged to do so (Nielsen and Webb, 2011), others use Skype for conferencing (Kharbach, 2012), and many even incorporate Twitter and Facebook as a regular part of their courses (Grisham, 2014). Future research could investigate what will become the 'norms' in these contexts of interaction and the pragmatic aspects at play in all of these various e-modes of communication. For example, a few specific questions might include the following: In contexts where students regularly text their teachers, how frequent are those texts as compared to e-mails? Do students use texts in ways and for purposes similar to those for which they use e-mail? What discourse elements characterize student-teacher interactions that take place through Skype? Do students use Skype to make requests, apologize, etc. and, if so, how do they go about this? And, what can be learned about student-teacher interaction that takes place in electronic contexts like Twitter and Facebook that can be much more public than private e-mail interactions?

What is clear from the present study is that students do not always follow e-mail norms preferred by some teachers. The effects of their 'transgressions' in these areas are challenging to identify and even harder to analyze. In the future, as e-mail will likely be replaced by new technologies, it is also likely that this will continue to be the case in whatever electronic contexts students and teachers communicate. Thus, researchers should further pursue these issues from both relational and pedagogical perspectives in e-mail contexts as well as in other e-modes of communication.

References

Absalom, M., & Pais Marden, M. (2004). Email communication and language learning at university – an Australian case study. *Computer Assisted Language Learning*, 17(3–4), 403–440. http://dx.doi.org/10.1080/0958822042000319647

Aijmer, K. (1996). *Conversational Routines in English*. London: Longman.

Allami, H., & Naeimi, A. (2011). A cross-linguistic study of refusals: an analysis of pragmatic competence development in Iranian EFL learners. *Journal of Pragmatics*, 43(1), 385–406. http://dx.doi.org/10.1016/j.pragma.2010.07.010

Ancarno, C. (2005). The style of academic e-mails and conventional letters: contrastive analysis of four conversational routines. *Ibérica*, 9, 103–122.

Anderson, D. (2002). Interfacing email tutoring: shaping an emergent literate practice. *Computers and Composition*, 19(1), 71–87. http://dx.doi.org/10.1016/S8755-4615(02)00081-6

Antón, M., & DiCamilla, F. (1998). Socio-cognitive functions of L1 collaborative interaction in the L2 classroom. *Canadian Modern Language Review*, 54(3), 314–342. http://dx.doi.org/10.3138/cmlr.54.3.314

Apte, M.L. (1974). 'Thank you' and South Asia languages: a comparativesociolinguistic study. *Linguistics*, 136, 67–89.

Aston, G. (1995). Say 'thank you': some pragmatic constraints in conversational closings. *Applied Linguistics*, 16(1), 57–86. http://dx.doi.org/10.1093/applin/16.1.57

Atamian, R., & DeMoville, W. (1998). Office hours – none. *College Teaching*, 46(1), 31–35. http://dx.doi.org/10.1080/87567559809596230

Baron, N.S. (1998). Letters by phone or speech by other means: the linguistics of email. *Language & Communication*, 18(2), 133–170. http://dx.doi.org/10.1016/S0271-5309(98)00005-6

Beebe, L.M., & Cummings, M.C. (1996). Natural speech act data versus written questionnaire data: how data collection method affects speech act performance. In S.M. Gass and J. Neu (Eds), *Speech Acts Across Cultures* 65–86. New York: Mouton de Gruyter.

Biesenbach-Lucas, S. (2005). Communication topics and strategies in e-mail consultation: comparison between American and international university students. *Language Learning & Technology*, 9(2), 24–46.

Biesenbach-Lucas, S. (2006). Making requests in e-mail: do cyber-consultations entail directness? Toward conventions in a new medium. In *Pragmatics and Language Learning* 51–107. Division of English as an International Language, Intensive English Institute, University of Illinois at Urbana-Champaign.

Biesenbach-Lucas, S. (2007). Students writing emails to faculty: an examination of e-politeness among native and non-native speakers of English. *Language Learning & Technology*, 11(2), 59–81.

Biesenbach-Lucas, S., & Weasenforth, D. (2002). Virtual office hours: negotiation strategies in electronic conferencing. *Computer Assisted Language Learning*, 15(2), 147–165. http://dx.doi.org/10.1076/call.15.2.147.8193

Bjørge, A.K. (2007). Power distance in English lingua franca email communication. *International Journal of Applied Linguistics*, 17(1), 60–80. http://dx.doi.org/10.1111/j.1473-4192.2007.00133.x

Bloch, J. (2002). Student/teacher interaction via email: the social context of internet discourse. *Journal of Second Language Writing*, 11(2), 117–134. http://dx.doi.org/10.1016/S1060-3743(02)00064-4

Blum-Kulka, S., House, J., & Kasper, G. (Eds) (1989). *Investigating Cross-Cultural Pragmatics: An Introductory Overview*. Cross-cultural pragmatics: Requests and apologies 1–34. Vol. XXXI. Norwood, NJ: Ablex.

Bretag, T. (2006). Using email to explore new subject positions for teachers and additional language learners. In K. Cadman & K. O'Regan (Eds), *Tales Out of School: Identity and English Language Learning. TESOL in Context*.

Brown, P., & Levinson, S.C. (1987). *Politeness: Some Universals in Language Usage*. Cambridge: Cambridge University Press.

Chambers, F. (1991). Promoting use of the target language in the classroom. *Language Learning Journal*, 4(1), 27–31. http://dx.doi.org/10.1080/09571739185200411

Chang, W.M., & Haugh, M. (2011). Evaluations of im/politeness of an intercultural apology. *Intercultural Pragmatics*, 8(3), 411–442. http://dx.doi.org/10.1515/iprg.2011.019

Chang, Y. (2010). 'I no say you say is boring': the development of pragmatic competence in L2 apology. *Language Sciences*, 32(3), 408–424. http://dx.doi.org/10.1016/j.langsci.2009.07.002

Chau, E. (2007). Learners' use of their first language in ESL classroom interactions. *TESOL in Context*, 16(2), 11–18.

Chen, C.E. (2006). The development of e-mail literacy: from writing to peers to writing to authority figures. *Language Learning & Technology*, 10(2), 35–55.

Chen, Y., Chen, C.D., & Chang, M.H. (2011). American and Chinese complaints: strategy use from a cross-cultural perspective. *Intercultural Pragmatics*, 8(2), 253–275. http://dx.doi.org/10.1515/iprg.2011.012

Cheng, S.W. (2010). A corpus-based approach to the study of speech act of thanking. *Concentric: Studies in Linguistics*, 36(2), 257–274.

Cohen, A.D. (1996) Investigating the production of speech act sets. In S. M. Gass and J. Neu (Eds), *Speech Acts across Cultures: Challenges to Communication in a Second Language* 21–43. Berlin: Mouton de Gruyer.

Cohen, A.D., & Shively, R.L. (2007). Acquisition of requests and apologies in Spanish and French: impact of study abroad and strategy-building intervention. *Modern Language Journal*, 91(2), 189–212. http://dx.doi.org/10.1111/j.1540-4781.2007.00540.x

Cook, V. (2001). Using the first language in the classroom. *Canadian Modern Language Review*, 57(3), 402–423. http://dx.doi.org/10.3138/cmlr.57.3.402

Cook, V. (2005) Basing teaching on the L2 user. In E. Llurda (Ed.), *Non-native Language Teachers: Perceptions, Challenges, and Contributions to the Profession* 47–61. Boston: Springer. http://dx.doi.org/10.1007/0-387-24565-0_4

Cook, V. (2012). 'Multi-competence' and 'Nativeness and language pedagogy. In C. Chapelle (Ed.), *The Encyclopedia of Applied Linguistics* 3768–3774 and 4173–4176. Oxford: Wiley-Blackwell.

Coulmas, F. (1981) Poison to your soul: thanks and apologies contrastively viewed. In F. Coulmas (Ed.) *Conversational Routine* 69–91. The Hague: Mouton de Gruyer. http://dx.doi.org/10.1515/9783110809145.69

Crouch, M.L., & Montecino, V. (1997) Cyberstress: asynchronous anxiety or worried in cyberspace – I wonder if my teacher got my email. TCC Online Conferences. Kapi'olani Community College. University of Hawai'i, Honolulu, HI.

Crystal, D. (2001). *Language and the Internet.* Cambridge: Cambridge University Press. http://dx.doi.org/10.1017/CBO9781139164771.

Crystal, D. (2006). *Language and the Internet* (2nd ed.). Cambridge: Cambridge University Press. http://dx.doi.org/10.1017/CBO9780511487002

Dalmau, M.S., & Gotor, H.C. (2007). From 'sorry very much' to 'I'm ever so sorry': acquisitional patterns in L2 apologies by Catalan learners of English. *Intercultural Pragmatics*, 4(2), 287–315. http://dx.doi.org/10.1515/IP.2007.014

Demeter, G. (2007). Role-plays as a data collection method for research on apology speech acts. *Simulation & Gaming*, 38(1), 83–90. http://dx.doi.org/10.1177/1046878106297880

Duff, P.A., & Polio, C.G. (1990). How much foreign language is there in the foreign language classroom? *Modern Language Journal*, 74(2), 154–166. http://dx.doi.org/10.1111/j.1540-4781.1990.tb02561.x

Economidou-Kogetsidis, M. (2011). 'Please answer me as soon as possible': pragmatic failure in non-native speakers' e-mail requests to faculty. *Journal of Pragmatics*, 43(13), 3193–3215. http://dx.doi.org/10.1016/j.pragma.2011.06.006

Edstrom, A. (2004). The L2 as language of instruction: teachers explore the competing tensions. *NECTFL Review*, 55, 26–32.

Edstrom, A. (2006). L1 use in the L2 classroom: one teacher's self-evaluation. *Canadian Modern Language Review*, 63(2), 275–292. http://dx.doi.org/10.3138/cmlr.63.2.275

Edstrom, A. (2007). Tracing one teacher's approach to communication throughout a semester of Spanish 101: belief meets practice. *Issues in Applied Linguistics*, 15(2), 149–168.

Edstrom, A. (2009). Teacher reflection as a strategy for evaluating L1/L2 use in the classroom. *Babylonia*, 1, 12–15.

Edstrom, A., & Ewald, J.D. (2006a). Student-teacher e-mail communication: an analysis of discourse patterns. National Meeting of the American Association for Applied Linguistics (AAAL and ACLA). Montréal, Canada. June, 2006.

Edstrom, A., & Ewald, J.D. (2006b). An analysis of e-mail discourse: windows into student-teacher interaction. Northeast Conference on the Teaching of Foreign Languages (Regional Meeting). New York City, New York. March, 2006.

Edwards, D. (2005). Moaning, whinging and laughing: the subjective side of complaints. *Discourse Studies*, 7(1), 5–29. http://dx.doi.org/10.1177/1461445605048765

Eisenstein, M., & Bodman, J. (1986). I very appreciate: expressions of gratitude by native and nonnative speakers of American English. *Applied Linguistics*, 7(2), 167–185. http://dx.doi.org/10.1093/applin/7.2.167

Eisenstein, M., & Bodman, J. (1993). Expressing gratitude in American English. In G. Kasper & S. Blum-Kulka (Eds) *Interlanguage Pragmatics* 64–81. New York: Oxford University Press.

Ewald, J.D. (2012). 'Can you tell me how to get there?': naturally-occurring versus role-play data in direction-giving. *Pragmatics*, *22*(1), 79–102. http://dx.doi.org/10.1075/prag.22.1.03ewa

Ewald, J.D. (2013). Another look at a speech act: An analysis of naturally-occurring student complaints sent through email. National Meeting of the American Association for Applied Linguistics (AAAL), Dallas, Texas. March, 2013.

Ewald, J.D., & Edstrom, A. (2006). Dear profesora: language students' use of e-mail to address attendance requirements. National Meeting of the American Association of the Teachers of Spanish and Portuguese (AATSP). Salamanca, Spain. July, 2006.

Ewald, J.D., & Edstrom, A. (2008). Language learners' e-mails: a context for teacher-student communication, L2 writing practice or both? National Meeting of the American Association for Applied Linguistics (AAAL), Washington, DC March, 2008.

Félix-Brasdefer, J.C. (2003) Validity in data collection methods in pragmatics research. In P. Kempchinsky and C. E. Piñeros (Eds), *Theory, Practice, and Acquisition. Papers from the 6th Hispanic Linguistics Symposium and the 5th Conference on the Acquisition of Spanish and Portuguese* 239–57. Somerville, MA: Cascadilla Press.

Félix-Brasdefer, J.C. (2007). Natural speech vs. elicited data: a comparison of natural and role play requests in Mexican Spanish.. *Spanish in Context*, *4*(2), 159–185. http://dx.doi.org/10.1075/sic.4.2.03fel

Gains, J. (1999). Electronic mail – a new style of communication or just a new medium? An investigation into the text features of e-mail. *English for Specific Purposes*, 18(1), 81–101. http://dx.doi.org/10.1016/S0889-4906(97)00051-3

Garrido, M.D.M. (2000). El correo electrónico en el aula: un ejemplo. *Cuadernos Cervantes*, *26*, 86–87.

Glater, J.D. February 21, 2006. "To: Professor@University.edu Subject: Why It's All About Me." *The New York Times*.

Grisham, L. April 9, 2014. "Teachers, Students and Social Media: Where is the Line?" *USA Today Network*.

Hannah, D.E., Glowacki-Dudka, M., & Conceicao-Runlee, S. (2000). *Synchronous and asynchronous learning. In 147 Practical Tips for Teaching Online Groups: Essentials of Web-Based Education*. Madison, WI: Atwood.

Hartford, B., & Mahboob, A. (2004). Models of discourse in the letter of complaint. *World Englishes*, 23(4), 585–600. http://dx.doi.org/10.1111/j.0083-2919.2004.00378.x

Hartford, B.S., & Bardovi-Harlig, K. (1996). 'At your earliest convenience': a study of written student requests to faculty. In L. F. Bouton (Ed.) *Pragmatics and Language Learning* 55–69. Monograph Series Volume 7. Urbana-Champaign, IL: University of Illinois, Division of English as an International Language.

Hassini, E. (2006). Student-instructor communication: the role of email. *Computers & Education*, 47(1), 29–40. http://dx.doi.org/10.1016/j.compedu.2004.08.014

Herring, S. (2002). Computer-mediated communication on the Internet. *Annual Review of Information Science & Technology*, 36(1), 109–168. http://dx.doi.org/10.1002/aris.1440360104

Hofstede, G. (2001). *Culture's consequences. Differences in work-related values*. Beverly Hills, CA: Sage. (Original work published 1980).

Hong, W. (2008). Effects of cultural background of college students on apology strategies. *International Journal of the Sociology of Language*, 189, 149–163.

House, J., & Kasper, G. (1981). Politeness markers in English and German. In F. Coulmas (Ed.), *Conversational Routine: Explorations in Standardized Communication Situations and Prepatterned Speech* 157–186. New York: Mouton.

Itakura, H. (2004). Changing cultural stereotypes through e-mail assisted foreign language learning. *System*, 32(1), 37–51. http://dx.doi.org/10.1016/j.system.2003.04.003

Jacobsson, M. (2002). Thank you and thanks in early modern English. *ICAME Journal*, 26, 63–80.

Jebahi, K. (2011). Tunisian university students' choice of apology strategies in a discourse completion task. *Journal of Pragmatics*, 43(2), 648–662. http://dx.doi.org/10.1016/j.pragma.2010.09.008

Jung, E.H. (2004) Interlanguage pragmatics: apology speech acts. In C. L. Moder and A. Martinovic-Zic (Eds), *Discourse Across Languages and Cultures* 99–116. Philadelphia: John Benjamins. http://dx.doi.org/10.1075/slcs.68.06jun

Kasanga, L.A., & Lwanga-Lumu, J. (2007). Cross-cultural linguistic realization of politeness: a study of apologies in English and Setswana. *Journal of Politeness Research*, 3(1), 65–92. http://dx.doi.org/10.1515/PR.2007.004

Kasper, G. & Blum-Kulka, S. (Eds). (1993). *Interlanguage Pragmatics*. New York, Oxford: Oxford University Press.

Kasper, G., & Dahl, M. (1991). *Research methods in interlanguage pragmatics*. Manoa: Hawaii University, Second Language Teaching and Curriculum Center.

Kharbach, M. (2012) *The Complete Guide to the Use of Skype in Education*. Educational Technology and Mobile Learning: A resource of educational web tools and mobile apps for teachers and educators. www.educatorstechnology.com/2012/06/complete-guide-to-use-of-skype-in.html

Knupsky, A.C., & Nagy-Bell, N.M. (2011). Dear professor: the influence of recipient sex and status on personalization and politeness in e-mail. *Journal of Language and Social Psychology*, 30(1), 103–113. http://dx.doi.org/10.1177/0261927X10387104

Kolowich, S. January 6, 2011. "How Will Students Communicate?" *Inside HigherEd*.

Laforest, M. (2002). Scenes of family life: complaining in everyday conversation. *Journal of Pragmatics*, 34(10–11), 1595–1620. http://dx.doi.org/10.1016/S0378-2166(02)00077-2

Lee, H.E., & Park, H.S. (2011). Why Koreans are more likely to favor 'apology' while Americans are more likely to favor 'thank you'. *Human Communication Research*, 37(1), 125–146. http://dx.doi.org/10.1111/j.1468-2958.2010.01396.x

Li, Y.L. (2000). Linguistic characteristics of ESL writing in task-based email activities. *System*, 28(2), 229–245. http://dx.doi.org/10.1016/S0346-251X(00)00009-9

Macaro, E. (2005) Codeswitching in the L2 classroom: a communication and learning strategy. In E. Llurda (Ed.), *Non-native Language Teachers: Perceptions, Challenges, and Contributions to the Profession* 63–84. Boston: Springer. http://dx.doi.org/10.1007/0-387-24565-0_5

Mach, T., & Ridder, S. (2003). E-mail requests. In K. Bardovi-Harlig and R. Mahan-Taylor. *Teaching Pragmatics*. Washington, DC: United States Department of State. Office of English Language Programs.

Marques, G. (2008). Establishing a continuum in spoken and written language in students' emails. *Systemic Functional Linguistics in Use. Odense Working Papers in Language and Communication*. 29: 564–76.

Martin, M.M., Myers, S.A., & Mottet, T.P. (1999). Students' motives for communicating with their instructors. *Communication Education*, 48(2), 155–164. http://dx.doi.org/10.1080/03634529909379163

Mason, M.A. (2010). E-Mail: The third shift. *Chronicle of Higher Education*, (July): 20.

Meier, A.J. (1997). What's the excuse?: Image repair in Austrian German. *Modern Language Journal*, 81(2), 197–208. http://dx.doi.org/10.1111/j.1540-4781.1997.tb01175.x

Mulamba, K. (2009). Social beliefs for the realization of the speech acts of apology and complaint as defined in Ciluba, French, and English. *Pragmatics*, 19(4), 543–564. http://dx.doi.org/10.1075/prag.19.4.03mul

Muniandy, A.V.A. (2002). Electronic-discourse (e-discourse): spoken, written or a new hybrid? *Prospect*, 17(3), 45–68.

Murphy, B., & Neu, J. (1996). My grade's too low: the speech act of complaining. In S. Gass & J. Neu (Eds) *Speech Acts Across Cultures: Challenges to Communication in a Second Language* 191–214. Berlin: Mouton de Gruyer.

Nielsen, L., & Webb, W. (2011). *Teaching Generation Text: Using Cell Phones to Enhance Learning*. San Francisco, CA: Jossey-Bass.

Noddings, N. (2005). What does it mean to Educate the WHOLE child? *Educational Leadership*, 63(1), 8–13.

O'Dowd, R. (2003). Understanding the 'other side': intercultural learning in a Spanish-English e-mail exchange. *Language Learning & Technology*, 7(2), 118–146.

Okamoto, S., & Robinson, W.P. (1997). Determinants of gratitude expressions in England. *Journal of Language and Social Psychology*, 16(4), 411–433. http://dx.doi.org/10.1177/0261927X970164003

Olshtain, E. (1989). Apologies across languages. In S. Blum-Kulka, J. House, & G. Kasper (Eds), *Cross-Cultural Pragmatics. Requests and Apologies* 155–73. Norwood: Alex Publishing Corporation.

Olshtain, E., & Cohen, A. (1983). Apology: a speech act set. In N. Wolfson and E. Judd (Eds) *Sociolinguistics and Language Acquisition* 18–35. Rowley, MA: Newbury House.

Olshtain, E., & Weinbach, L. (1987). Complaints: A study of speech act behavior among native and non-native speakers of Hebrew. In J. Verschueren & M. Bertucelli-Papi (Eds), *The Pragmatic Perspective* 195–208. Amsterdam: John Benjamins.

Pérez, F.J.D. (2005). The speech act of thanking in English. Differences between native and non-native speakers' behaviour. *Revista de Filología Inglesa*, 26, 91–101.

Pérez, L. (2000). Electronic mail, an extension of my Spanish class boundaries. *Cincinnati Romance Review*, 19, 138–145.

Pirie, R. (2000). Ask an expert: email etiquette_e-mail effectiveness. *CA Magazine (Toronto)*, 133, 11.

Poling, D.J. (1994). E-Mail as an effective teaching supplement. *Educational Technology,* 34(5): 53–55.

Polio, C., & Duff, P. (1994). Teachers' language use in university foreign language classrooms: A qualitative analysis of English and target language alternation. *Modern Language Journal,* 78(3), 313–326. http://dx.doi.org/10.1111/j.1540-4781.1994.tb02045.x

Porath, S. (2011). Text messaging and teenagers: a review of the literature. *Journal of the Research Center for Educational Technology,* 87(7), 86–99.

Richtel, M. (2010). E-mail gets an instant makeover. *The New York Times* December 20.

Rife, M.C. (2007). The Professional E-mail Assignment, or, whatsyername@howyadoin. com. *Teaching English in the Two-Year College,* 34(3), 264–270.

Rintell, E., & Mitchell, C. J. (1989). Studying requests and apologies: An inquiry into method. In S. Blum-Kulka, J. House, & G. Kasper (Eds), *Cross-cultural Pragmatics,* 248–272. Norwood, NJ: Ablex.

Rod, Z.M., & Eslami-Rasekh, Z. (2005) E-mail discourse of native and non-native TESOL graduate students: openings. Paper presented at the meeting of *Pragmatics and language learning,* April, 2005, Bloomington, IN.

Rose, J.M. (2004). 'Be seeing u' in unfamiliar places: ESL writers, e-mail epistolaries, and critical computer literacy. *Computers and Composition: An International Journal,* 21(2), 237–249. http://dx.doi.org/10.1016/j.compcom.2004.02.002

Ruzaitė, J., & Čubajevaitė, L. (2007). Apologies in business communication. [Eesti Rakenduslingvistika Ühingu aastaraamat]. *Estonian Papers in Applied Linguistics,* 3, 67–81.

Samar, R.G., Navidinia, H., & Mehrani, M.B. (2010). Communication purposes and strategies in email communication: a contrastive analysis between Iranian and American students. *International Journal of Language Studies,* 4(3), 55–72.

Schauer, G.A., & Adolphs, S. (2006). Expressions of gratitude in corpus and DCT data: vocabulary, formulaic sequences, and pedagogy. *System,* 34(1), 119–134. http://dx.doi. org/10.1016/j.system.2005.09.003

Sciubba, M.E. (2010). Salutations, openings and closings in today academic emails. *Studi Italiani di Linguistica Teorica e Applicata,* 39(2), 243–264.

Scott, M.B., & Lyman, S.M. (1968). Accounts. *American Sociological Review,* 33(1), 46–62. http://dx.doi.org/10.2307/2092239

Scott, V.M., & De la Fuente, M.J. (2008). What is the problem? L2 learners' use of the L1 during consciousness-raising form-focused tasks. *Modern Language Journal,* 92(1), 100–113. http://dx.doi.org/10.1111/j.1540-4781.2008.00689.x

Shea, V. (1994). *Netiquette.* San Francisco: Albion.

Sheer, V.C., & Fung, T.K. (2007). Can email communication enhance professor-student relationship and student evaluation of professor?: some empirical evidence. *Journal of Educational Computing Research,* 37(3), 289–306. http://dx.doi.org/10.2190/ EC.37.3.d

Shively, R. L. and Cohen, A. D. (2008) Development of Spanish requests and apologies during study abroad. *Ikala, revista de lenguaje y cultura* 13(20):57–118.

Stephens, K.K., Houser, M.L., & Cowan, R.L. (2009). R u able to meat me: the impact of students' overly casual email messages to instructors. *Communication Education*, 58(3), 303–326. http://dx.doi.org/10.1080/03634520802582598

Storch, N., & Wigglesworth, G. (2003). Is there a role for the use of the L1 in an L2 setting? *TESOL Quarterly*, 37(4), 760–770. http://dx.doi.org/10.2307/3588224

Strenski, E., Feagin, C.O., & Singer, J.A. (2005). Email small group peer review revisited. *Computers and Composition*, 22(2), 191–208. http://dx.doi.org/10.1016/j.compcom.2005.02.005

Swain, M., & Lapkin, S. (2000). Task-based second language learning: The uses of the first language. *Language Teaching Research*, 4(3), 251–274. http://dx.doi.org/10.1177/136216880000400304

Snyder, C.R., Higgins, R.L., & Stucky, R.J. (1983). *Excuses. Masquerades in Search of Grace*. New York: John Wiley & Sons.

Tannen, D. (2013). The medium is the metamessage: conversational style in new media interaction. In D. Tannen and A.M. Trester (Eds) *Discourse 2.0* 99–118. Washington, DC: Georgetown University Press.

Thoms, J., Liao, J., & Szustak, A. (2005). The use of L1 in an L2 on-line chat activity. *Canadian Modern Language Review*, 62(1), 161–182. http://dx.doi.org/10.3138/cmlr.62.1.161

Tran, G.Q. (2002). Pragmatic and discourse transfer in complaining. *Melbourne Papers in Linguistics and Applied Linguistics*, 2(2), 71–97.

Turnbull, M. (2001). There is a role for the L1 in second and foreign language teaching, but .... *Canadian Modern Language Review*, 57(4), 531–540. http://dx.doi.org/10.3138/cmlr.57.4.531

Turnbull, M., & Dailey-O'Cain, J. (2009). *First Language Use in Second and Foreign Language Learning*. Clevedon: Multilingual Matters.

Vásquez, C. (2011). Complaints online: the case of *TripAdvisor*. *Journal of Pragmatics*, 43(6), 1707–1717. http://dx.doi.org/10.1016/j.pragma.2010.11.007

Wagner, L.C., & Roebuck, R. (2010). Apologizing in Cuernavaca, Mexico and Panama City, Panama: a cross-cultural comparison of positive-and negative-politeness strategies. *Spanish in Context*, 7(2), 254–278. http://dx.doi.org/10.1075/sic.7.2.05wag

Waldeck, J.H., Kearney, P., & Plax, T.G. (2001). Teacher e-mail message strategies and students' willingness to communicate online. *Journal of Applied Communication Research*, 29(1), 54–70. http://dx.doi.org/10.1080/00909880128099

Weinstock, J.A. (2004). Respond now! E-mail, acceleration, and a pedagogy of patience. *Pedagogy*, 4(3), 365–384. http://dx.doi.org/10.1215/15314200-4-3-365

Weiss, M., & Hanson-Baldauf, D. (2008). E-mail in academia: expectations, use, and instructional impact. *EDUCAUSE Quarterly*, 31(1): 42–50.

Worrells, D. S. (2001). Asynchronous distance learning: e-mail attachments used as the medium for assigned coursework. *ATEA Journal*: 29(2): 4–6.

Index

Lightning Source UK Ltd.
Milton Keynes UK
UKOW06f1023280116

267285UK00003B/85/P